The Europeans

Richard Mayne

THE
EUROPEANS
Who are we?

WEIDENFELD AND NICOLSON
5 Winsley Street London W1

Copyright © 1972 by Richard Mayne

To Zoë

ISBN 0 297 99424 7

Printed in Great Britain by
Willmer Brothers Limited, Birkenhead

Contents

1

In Search of a Tribe

> "You intend to return to Europe and resume your irregular manner of life?" Mr Wentworth inquired.
> "I can't say I intend. But it's very likely I shall go back to Europe. After all, I am a European. I feel that, you know."
>
> HENRY JAMES, *The Europeans*

THE Europeans? What Europeans?

Europe today may be seeking unity; but its inhabitants remain divided. In Western Europe alone, an area one-third the size of the United States, they belong to a score of countries with half-a-dozen different political systems. They use fifteen national currencies. They speak at least eleven languages, with a wide variety of dialects and local accents. In several countries, cultural minorities are fighting for independence; in almost all, violent protesters have challenged the *status quo*. With bloodshed in Ulster, babel in Switzerland and Belgium, dictatorship in Greece, Spain, and Portugal, political insecurity in Italy, and monetary confusion in the Common Market, a visitor from Mars or America might well ask whether "the Europeans" have any identity at all.

At one time, the answer would have been simple. The old Europe of spas and ballrooms, courts and carriages, Grand

I

Tours and petty principalities, had its own brittle cultural unity and a cosmopolitan élite. The artful Old Worldlings of Henry James's novel, set in the 1840s, were perhaps its last representatives. Just a hundred years earlier, Voltaire had argued that "Christian Europeans are what the Greeks once were: they go to war with each other; but in their disagreements they retain so much decorum, and usually so much politeness, that when a Frenchman, an Englishman, and a German meet they often seem like natives of the same town." French was the language, Reason the new faith, of that powdered and bewigged fraternity; but there were deeper reasons why European countries seemed alike. All were still mainly agricultural. All had a largely peasant population – the base of a social pyramid topped by the monarchy and sanctioned by the Church. The urban middle classes were important, and growing more so as commerce and industry developed; but political power, throughout much of Europe, still lay with an aristocracy that retained mediaeval titles and trappings. By the end of the eighteenth century, dramatic changes were overdue; yet even Edmund Burke, himself a critic of the cosmopolitan Enlightenment, remarked nearly a decade after the French Revolution that "no citizen of Europe can be altogether an exile in any part of it."

Between Burke's day and ours stand the scarred monuments of nationalism. This is more than a matter of loyalty to the flag. Such symbols are still potent, even when they appear on shopping-bags or avant-garde canvases: in America, middle-aged citizens are still distressed when student rebels burn the star-spangled banner, and rebels still bother to burn it; in France, the authorities still severely punish drunken sailors who douse the sacred flame at the Étoile. But national feeling springs from other sources also. Some are ideological. The French Revolutionary armies waved the tricolor; but they also preached liberty, equality, and fraternity, whatever they may have practised. Italy's nationalist Risorgimento was also a fight against autocracy: Mazzini and Garibaldi were revolutionaries, whatever might be said of Cavour. Similar feelings persisted in World War I, and were predominant in World War II, when democratic nations saw themselves as bastions of freedom against totalitarian régimes. Nationalism, then, was also "functional", in the language of political scientists: involvement in the national system conferred rewards and advantages. At the same time, it was "normative", implying at a primitive level blind conformity, and in a more sophisticated sense acceptance of the state's multiple demands.

It might be thought that nationalism now had been discredited. War has been one of its offshoots; and since the beginning of recorded history war has killed almost as many men, women, and children as now inhabit the earth. With every century, wars have grown more costly. In the eighteenth century, they claimed 5½ million victims; in the nineteenth, 16 million; in the twentieth, more than 75 million. Modern weapons have stripped the glamour from patriotism of the old school: much of its rhetoric is defunct. Listening today to World War I speeches, or to newsreel commentaries on World War II, is an astonishing reminder of the bombast once taken for granted. Did we ever really believe those stirring *Boys' Own Paper* voices ringing out above the military marches, chronicling mass slaughter in metaphors from the cricket-field?

The tone has changed; but in many places the message remains the same. In the Middle East, in Africa, Asia, and Latin America, men are still ready to die – and kill – for "national liberation". Hijackers and urban guerrillas replay the Risorgimento with different firearms and vocabulary, but similar ideology and appearance. To many Europeans, who know the suffering that nationalism brought to their own continent, the spectacle is tragic. But they also know how much easier it is to have civilized scruples when one is privileged and rich. Even in Europe, moreover, nationalism is still a living force. Passion has given way to habit; but if national feelings have become less explicit and violent, they are now even more pervasive. One reason is the multiplication, in our century, of contacts between the citizen and the nation-state.

In *laissez-faire* economies, with fairly primitive technology and slow communications, daily experience tended to be local. The town or the village was the first focus of politics and society. Even Grand Tourists were as much concerned with the inn or the region as with the country they happened to be in: customs and immigration officials met them at the city gates. Now, when the state has assumed so many responsibilities – for economic policy, industrial relations, and social welfare of many kinds – there are continual reminders that "we" are British, French, German, or Italians, rather than Mancunians, Dijonnais, Münchner. or Milanesi, still less citizens of Europe or of the world. The press, radio, and television – even where they are regional – strengthen national self-consciousness by their very existence, as well as by their language and content. So, above all, does education, "universal" in its social scope, but still deeply national in its political assumptions.

Walter Hallstein, the first President of the Common Market Commission, once confessed that as a schoolboy in Mainz he had been taught to regard the French as Germany's "hereditary enemies". This was an extreme instance; but equally chauvinist doctrines were current in France, not all of them traceable to Nicholas Chauvin. Nor was Britain exempt, even a generation later. As a child, I went to a junior day school in the suburbs of London; it had also been attended, I found later, by "Cassandra" of the *Daily Mirror*. It was a good but modest establishment, in a grey Victorian house with its name on a big brass plate by the privet hedge. Originally it had been known as "Frankfort House"; then, no doubt as a sop to anti-German feelings in World War I, the name had been changed to "Franklin House". But instead of ordering a new name-plate, the school had simply added a small brass strip with the letters LIN to cover the original FORT. Whether this was an economy measure or a tacit protest against the alteration, we never knew: but the mutilated nameplate was a daily reminder that there was something suspect about Frankfort. One of the teachers in the same school, a harassed young woman who seemed to her ten-year-old pupils an omniscient elderly sage, carried patriotism still further. The British, she told us, were pre-eminent in the world because their temperate island climate saved them from continental sloth.

So much for geography. History, there and elsewhere, was no less insular. Anglo-Dutch rivalry, the Hundred Years' War, the struggle against Napoleon, and World War I, became patriotic adventure-stories – as they did in Holland, France, and Germany; but more insidious in England was the David-and-Goliath moral implicit in certain favourite episodes. At the battles of Crécy and Agincourt, the tried, trusty, unpretentious British longbowmen had roundly defeated the top-heavy, armour-clad French cavalry and the over-elaborate continental crossbow. At the time of the Armada, the efficient matter-of-fact Drake with his small fast ships had punctured the pride and pomp of the huge, costly, and ornate Spanish galleons. Both tales were true; but as ethical fables they were especially consoling to the inhabitants of a small island, still rather puritanical and no longer supreme in the world. Never mind the size and wealth of America, the industrial efficiency of Germany, the sophisticated elegance of France: manly simplicity and native skill could outdo all overblown foreign pretensions. This was the lesson; it almost gave moral stature to the plainness of British cooking. How much did it contribute to Britain's stubborn courage in 1940 and 1941, when she stood virtually alone against the Nazi and Fascist conquerors of continental Europe? How much, later, did it bolster the belief that she could stand alone against the competition of the world's economic giants?

Travel might have been expected to offset such nationally oriented teaching. Instead, it often narrowed the mind. The story of the French schoolboy in London, puzzled because the streets and railway stations were named after defeats, not victories, is no doubt apocryphal; but many British tourists, whose chief memories of "history" are of Tudor and Stuart politics, have been just as baffled by the bearded effigies in foreign squares, as well as by the dates so often used in foreign street-names. If even inhabitants of Paris and Rome are no longer certain what happened on August 25, September 4 or 20, or November 4, visitors are even less so. They leave with the vague impression that their hosts are obsessed by long-forgotten convulsions – overlooking the Inkerman Roads and Plevna Crescents nearer home.

Even standard works of reference reinforce national prejudice. Who invented radio – the cinema – aircraft – television? Clerk Maxwell, Hertz, or Marconi? William Friese-Greene, or the Lumière brothers? Sir George Cayley, Montgolfier, or Graf Zeppelin? Baird, Zworykin, or Rosing? The answers often depend on the nationality of the encyclopaedias. All agree that such discoveries are a cumulative process, with many inventors groping towards similar goals; but each will if necessary unearth an obscure pioneer of the right nationality, "without whose efforts subsequent progress might have been much slower", or "whose designs, although never given a thorough trial [after the first few explosions], contained in embryo much that was to come [including further explosions]."

With information like this in the classroom and the library, what could be more natural than prejudice in the playground and the home? Words like "Frog", "Hun", and "Wop", or *Rosbif*, *Boche*, and *Macaroni*, are now mainly fossils of translators' slang; but the feeling behind them lingers. "The French", "the Germans", "the Italians" – each carries with it an alienating overtone. It may be a sense of superiority, or only a sense of difference: in either case it assumes that all members of the same nation have more in common, in the last resort, than any is likely to have with a "foreigner". Put so baldly, this sounds absurd. Animal-lovers or revolutionary students are surely closer to their counterparts in other countries than to big-game hunters or wealthy businessmen in their own. Yet all are still half-expected to share national characteristics, national priorities, and national preoccupations.

6

In Search of a Tribe

> I often think it's comical
> How Nature always does contrive
> That every boy and every gal,
> That's born into the world alive,
> Is either a little Liberal,
> Or else a little Conservative!

wrote W. S. Gilbert in *Iolanthe*. His audiences laughed at the quaint conceit. But no one in 1882 saw anything comical in babies being born little Englishmen or little Frenchmen. Political parties were artifacts. Nations, it seemed, were not.

Today, this is less self-evident. The nation can now be seen as one among many social groups – families, clubs, churches, business firms, trade unions, political parties, schools, universities, professional associations, local and regional councils, military alliances, and international organizations. The powers and duties of the nation-state, and its rôle in the life of citizens, have certainly grown since *Iolanthe;* but its ability to cope with its growing tasks has hardly kept pace with change.

Present-day technology is no respecter of frontiers. Aircraft, spacecraft, and missiles ignore them; so does radio; so, increasingly, does television; so does pollution. International finance finds ways to cross them; so do multinational corporations, and trade unions are only more slowly following suit. For many of today's purposes – defence, research and development, and adequate aid to the world's poor and hungry – the nation-states that Europeans have inherited from the past are too small to be effective alone. And if only to reassert democratic control over forces that more and more transcend the national dimension, governments are obliged to come together. A united world is at present beyond their reach. It might in any case prove forbiddingly top-heavy. But the delegation of some national sovereignty to larger groupings is certainly feasible. On a limited scale, it has already begun.

Since 1945, most Western nations have accepted until – recently – the code of good conduct laid down by the International Monetary Fund. Since 1947, they have curbed their own freedom in commercial policy by respecting the General Agreement on Tariffs and Trade. Since 1949, they have entrusted their own defence to the Atlantic Alliance. Partly as a result, they have enjoyed unique prosperity and comparative peace.

In western Europe, the process has gone still further. Recognizing that individually they are now no match for the world's giants, a number of European countries have pledged themselves to unity. They began by gradually removing the trade barriers that once divided them, making possible the free movement of goods, people, and money. They are now trying to treat their once separate economies as a single whole. To help them, they have devised rules of fair play and transnational institutions. The official name of the game is the European Economic Community or "Common Market". Some believe that it will one day form the basis of a United States of Europe.

To apply this proud, daunting, and ambiguous phrase to the present imperfect machinery of the Common Market would obviously be premature. Whether the Community will ever move on from economics to foreign policy and defence, and at length to a federation or even a confederation, is still an open question, to be decided by its members in the future. But even now, in the words of the Common Market treaty, its aim is "an ever closer union"; and some fear that by helping to build it they may be committed to a process too radical to stop.

A united Europe may have the chance of enjoying more wealth, more security, and more world influence. If European nations remained divided, each might merely preserve its formal "sovereignty" while its real freedom of action ebbed away. But if a political community is one day to be built in western Europe, this will take more than speeches, treaties, intergovernmental meetings, or exhortatory books. European unity, in however loose a confederation, can only come about and endure if Europeans themselves share a sense of solidarity, common loyalty, and mutual trust.

8

Loyalty to a continent – or even to half of it – is not easily felt. In the United States of America, racial injustice and the Vietnam war have shown how frail the state of the Union still is. Yet Americans have understandably tried as hard as anyone to stamp a sense of identity on their "nation of immigrants", putting the flag in the classroom, having children recite the Declaration of Independence, neglecting or discouraging Cajun French and other minority languages, and even calling anti-social activities "un-American".

Europeans have often smiled at this curious use of language; but some of them use the words "Europe" and "European" no less eccentrically. "Europe" has become a one-word cliché, too often restricted to mean only western Europe, or only the six founder-members of the Common Market. In Britain, countless orators have debated whether or not to "go into Europe" – as if they were not there already, or as if signing the Common Market treaty would set off some supranational crane to lift the British Isles on to the mainland. "The European idea" has come to mean the idea of unity – as if Europeans had had no other; and some of its champions have even tried to corner for "European civilization" such human values as freedom, justice, equality, and truthfulness.

Arrogance of this sort is certainly misplaced. Bad ethics and worse history, it would not even be effective cement. In the nineteenth century, when Italians and Germans were trying to weld principalities together into nations, they could appeal to patriotic sentiment; but today it would surely be futile to expect Europeans to break their national habits of mind by feeling for Europe what Mazzini felt for Italy or Fichte for Germany. Nor is this all. Nationalism would still be nationalism if it were transposed to a European scale. And in a world where racial tension, poverty, greed, sloth, fear, and resentment threaten the survival of civilization, it would be irresponsible to give any further sanction to a divisive force that in other parts of the world is still as strong as it was in Europe a century ago.

But if "European nationalism", as sometimes preached by

French and other Gaullists, is a lost cause that few reasonable people would want to revive, there is some sense in trying to identify what, if anything, Europeans have in common. Not, that is, the "Europeans" of Henry James, vanished for ever into the pump-rooms. Not the surviving "white" colonists of tropical regions, nursed in precarious privilege like pre-Revolutionary *seigneurs*. Not the once "new Europeans" of the 1950s and early 1960s, newly affluent, naïvely confident, scarcely yet questioning their shiny consumer society. Not – or not only – the "European" militants, sometimes piously styled "good Europeans" or, in Britain, given the ramshackle nickname "marketeers". Instead, the tribe we are seeking is that of the European Community in all its variety – from North Sea trawlermen to Parisian high civil servants, from dapper German businessmen to the peasants of southern Italy.

Already, their separate governments are behaving as if all these people shared some sense of identity greater than that which potentially unites mankind. What is its objective basis? Has Europe, so long divided, as much natural unity as any of its separate nations? Is there any truth in the metaphor that Europeans form a family? Is language a permanent barrier between them? Is national prejudice too deep-rooted to die? Is "national character" a reality? Are professional "Europeans" harbingers of the future? Is there a real "European tradition" – or is this just another comforting European myth?

Some of the answers to these questions depend upon choices to be made today or tomorrow: in some respects, the Europeans hold their future in their own hands. Others, however, lie very deep in Europe's past. It may be best to begin with those that are as old as the hills.

2

A Promontory of Asia

On a round ball
A workeman that hath copies by, can lay
An Europe, Afrique, and an Asia,
And quickly make that, which was nothing, *All*.

JOHN DONNE, "A Valediction: Of Weeping"

How firm is *terra firma*? At one time, it was thought that the earth we walk on was a hollow crust enclosing a molten core, and that its surface had cracked and wrinkled into valleys and mountains as the globe gradually cooled. This was perhaps a lay version of religious cosmology. The crust represented the finite imperfect world of man, between Fra Angelico's blue empyrean and Hieronymus Bosch's fiery hell.

Today, the picture looks more complex. The earth's core is now thought to be a solid over 6,000 miles in diameter – probably an alloy of iron and nickel, whose magnetic attraction, among other things, prevents our drifting weightlessly into space. Around it is a crust, or a series of crusts, some 700 miles thick. The inferno still rages. A day's mule-ride down the Grand Canyon can take the December visitor from bitter cold and snow at Bright Angel Point on the North

Rim to a warm riverside picnic at the bottom. In mines, deep boreholes, and tunnels like that through Mont Blanc, the temperature of the rock increases by about 1°C. every 100 feet down. The increase seems to taper off at a depth of some sixty miles – ten times that of the deepest ocean; but even there the heat is probably about 1,500°C., partly a remnant of the earth's beginnings, and partly the product of radioactivity. At atmospheric pressure, such a temperature would melt any rock; but the pressure at this depth holds most of it rigid. Only where fissures occur does the rock turn into magma and erupt to the surface – scattering millions of tons of fragments and lava, and sometimes killing many thousands of people, as at Vesuvius, Bandai-san, Krakatoa, Mont Pelée, Messina, or Paricutín.

Today's volcanoes appear to be the survivors of subterranean storms now dying or dormant, which in remoter times helped shape the surface of our earth. But it may also be that under the earth's topmost crust, at a depth of some forty miles, there lies a layer of more plastic rock, with a high proportion of silica and magnesia, on which the lighter blocks that form the continents "float" like icebergs in a sea. If so, this might substantiate the theory of "continental drift" put forward in the 1920s by the German geologist Wegener. Noticing that the earth's present five continents could be fitted together like a crude and gigantic jigsaw puzzle, he suggested that some 250 million years ago they may have formed a single compact block, more or less heart-shaped and surrounded by sea. Only later, he thought, had they drifted apart to assume their present positions. Attractive as this theory may be, it remains hard to verify. All that is certain is that the shape as well as the height of today's dry land has varied very greatly throughout the æons of geological time, and that present-day Europe, like the other continents, still bears countless traces of its remote and complex origins.

One initially puzzling feature of geology is its habit of turning chronology upside-down. Tables of geological time, that is, put the latest periods at the top, rather like those lists of stations in the London Underground where travellers are expected to start reading at the bottom and work their way up. The reason is fairly obvious: the older rocks are usually considered to underlie the later, like pagan remnants beneath the foundations of a Christian church. The convention goes back (or down) as far as the so-called "father of English geology", William Smith, who in the early nineteenth century produced a table of fossil-bearing strata, descending from London clay through chalk, greensand, oolite, lias, new red sandstone, coal measures, and old red sandstone, to the curiously-named Greywacke rocks. Smith's classification has long been superseded: the Greywacke rocks, in particular, soon proved to be very much more than an undifferentiated, gritty, primeval sludge. But although European and other geologists now use more sophisticated tables, they still put the oldest at the bottom; and in one respect the practice is misleading. Europe, like the rest of our planet, was not formed like a simple layer-cake: much of it was kneaded like dough. At least four times, at intervals of roughly 150 million years, immense upheavals raised a series of mountain ranges, each to be later worn and weathered, and all but the most recent squeezed by the next slow convulsion. In this fourfold process, Europe acquired some of the physical features that in turn have helped to mould its inhabitants.

Scandinavia has a reputation for toughness that it well deserves. Most of the oldest and hardest surface bedrock in Europe lies in Finland, Sweden, parts of Norway, and the Danish island of Bornholm – lands of granite and layered gneiss and schists that date from the first and longest of the earth's great eras, the Archaean, well over 600 million years ago. Once, they probably extended into the Atlantic and Arctic Oceans and south-east into what is now Russia. Over time, they warped and stretched into mountains, which wore away gradually and were invaded by shallow seas, bearing sediment and life. As the sediment solidified, it too heaved and folded into a vast mountain-range, running from present-day Norway to Scotland, across to Greenland, and perhaps as far as Canada. Later, most of this was eroded away. It took 400 million years of further turmoil, including great gushes of lava, to reduce the northern world to something more like its present shape. Iceland arose, much bigger than now; Norway's cliffs fell sharply away to the west; to the east, the land was slowly lifted.

That past is remote: but its traces still linger. Along many of the western coasts of Europe there are legends of vanished kingdoms, swallowed up by the waves. In the early mediaeval Norwegian *Edda*, the finest poem describes the destruction of the world: the sun turns black, the earth sinks into the sea, hot stars fall from heaven, and fire leaps high into the air.

Outside Scandinavia, only a fragment of Europe's oldest rock now lies near the surface – the Outer Hebrides and the strip of mainland facing them, known collectively as "the ancient Lewisian foreland". This and its much larger Scandinavian counterpart, "the Fenno-Scandinavian shield", were the fulcrum on which later forces thrust, to bend, compress, and lever Europe into its existing forms.

The second great upheaval took place some 150 million years after the first – about 450 million years ago, in the middle of the Palaeozoic era, the second main segment of geological time. This was the "Caledonian" system of foldings in the earth's surface, so called because it formed the Highlands and Southern Uplands of Scotland – although it also shaped the Lake District, the Welsh Massif, and the Massifs of Donegal and Mayo, south-east Ulster, and Wicklow and Wexford, as well as parts of Scandinavia and the downfold that became the Donets Basin in the present USSR. The Caledonian mountains have narrow folds, a granite core, and steeply tilted sedimentaries – a technical description that in some ways fits their inhabitants. In Ireland, especially, there are also later volcanic effects like the "Giant's Causeway", that spectacular promontory of 40,000 basalt columns stepping westward from the coast of Antrim and recalling the similar "Devil's Post Pile" in California.

During the interval before the next upheaval, heavy rainfall raised enormous forests of tree ferns over much of western Europe, especially in what are now the British Isles, northern France, the Low Countries, and north Germany. When these forests finally silted over, coal was formed, and the future Black Country took shape. Again, the interval lasted about 150 million years.

Then, mainly to the south of the Caledonian folding, came the third great European convulsion, the "Hercynian". This name was first used by Julius Caesar in his *Conquest of Gaul*. He spoke there of "the Hercynian Forest", and referred to "Eratosthenes and other Greeks, who call it Orcynia." "It is so wide," he added, "that it takes a lightly-equipped traveller nine days to cross." It covered, he thought, the whole area from the Black Forest to Bohemia. The Hercynian upheaval, however, was even more extensive: it affected areas as far west as the British Isles and the Iberian Peninsula, as far north as the Low Countries, and as far east as the Balkans and Russia. Its traces today are very varied, since time, wind, water, sediment, and further mineral turmoil have worn down, cracked, silted, and sunk what was once a mountain-range spanning Europe like a ruckled carpet. Most obvious today are those of its worn remnants that have been lifted to form plateaux – in southern Ireland, Wales, Devon and Cornwall, Brittany, the Massif Central, the Vosges, and the Black Forest. In places, smaller disturbances caused not only folds but also faults or fractures, as at Cross Fell in the Pennines; and some of the folds brought coal close to the surface.

A further 200 million years went by before the fourth and latest phase of European mountain-making. Then, once more, titanic pressure built up, partly the result of disturbances further south. The sediments that formed the bed of what was to be narrowed into the Mediterranean were now squeezed and buckled against the stumps of the Hercynian range. Rising, they became Europe's youngest system of mountains, the Alpine. Named for its best-known components, this includes the Pyrenees, the Apennines, the Tatra, the Carpathians, and the Caucasus. Their formation caused further up-heavals in the Hercynian range: new cracks appeared in it; a new fold became the Paris Basin and the Weald of Kent; in the far north, the land was broken up again, and the Atlantic flooded further in. The Apine system itself has since been levered higher into spectacular crests and crags. Erosion has had less time to work on them than on Europe's older mountains: it has not yet smoothed them, but it has carved out dramatically steep cliffs. Here and there, harder rock has been forced up into plateaux like the Spanish Meseta; elsewhere, it has been crushed down to form a seabed like that of the Adriatic or a great inland hollow like the Hungarian plain.

This last upheaval ended about 100 million years ago. If periodicity were any guide, another might be expected in 50 or 100 million years' time. Meanwhile, Europe's landscape has been further sculpted and modelled by erosion and silting; and quite late in geological time, between about 600,000 and 120,000 years ago, normal erosion by water was redoubled by the action of ice.

Ice spread from two main centres – one along the mountains of Scandinavia, the other in the Alps. Four times in some areas, at intervals ranging from 30,000 to 200,000 years, the glaciers expanded and contracted. At their most extensive, they covered all of Scandinavia, the North Sea, the Baltic, northern Russia, north Germany, the Netherlands, all the British Isles except the southern counties of England, most of Switzerland, and the French, Italian, and Austrian Alps. In many places, the ice was over 10,000 feet thick. Advancing and retreating, it ground away mountains, reducing the Alps to about half their previous height; it rasped the plains, scooped out lakes, and scraped out valleys, massaging the land with its changing weight. In the intervals between the coldest spells, both water and wind added their share to the landscape. Floods from the receding glaciers washed over large areas a fine-ground clay, interspersed with smooth stones, typical of East Anglia; dry winds spread a richer dust that may have become the greyish loam of the valleys further south. Nor, even now, is the work of the glaciers over. Conceivably, within some 80,000 years, they might recur. As it is, some remain – in Switzerland, for instance, and the Pyrenees. In Iceland, they still coexist with hot springs and volcanoes, sometimes producing a "glacier burst" when a volcano erupts under the ice. In Finland and Sweden, the shrinking of the glaciers, which still continues, has caused the land to rise about a foot in thirty years on parts of the Bothnian coast.

To all these forces Europe owes its character – small, moderate, changeable, varied, and rich.

Of all the continents, Europe is bigger only than Australia. It is also, especially in its western regions, the most intermingled with the sea. In the Middle West of America, more than 1,000 miles from either ocean, there are still many people who have never seen a seashore. Few places in Europe are more than 500 miles from one: the main exception is in central Russia. In this sense, Europe is a promontory of Asia, a land of islands and estuaries, peninsulas and inlets, with the sea stealing in around many miles of sandy, rocky, gentle, or precipitous shores.

This is not merely picturesque to look at: it is also a key to Europe's nature. Just as the European landscape has no towering Andes or Himalayas, and the surrounding ocean no Pacific depths, so since the most recent ice age the European climate has known no truly Arctic cold and no Saharan or New Mexican heat. January temperatures in Europe vary between – 8.5° C. in the north-east and 10° at the Mediterranean, rising in July to about 16° round the North Sea and about 27° in the south. By far the greatest climatic extremes occur in the far north and the landlocked areas to the east. Elsewhere, the sea acts as a thermostat.

It used to be thought – by Benjamin Franklin among others – that the seas round Europe were warmed by the Gulf Stream, the strong current from the Gulf of Mexico that moves up America's eastern seaboard to Newfoundland, where it meets the cold Labrador Current from the north. But although the prevailing westerly winds blow a surface current – the "north Atlantic drift" – towards Europe, a more likely source of her warm seas is an irregular northward drift of tropical waters, twisted north-eastward by the rotation of the earth and replaced by Arctic waters, which on crossing the equator are similarly twisted west. The warm tide has little effect on the Mediterranean, directly heated by the sun; nor does it much influence the fresher and colder Baltic, parts of which freeze every winter. But elsewhere around Europe the sea exerts a moderating influence, storing heat and cold and lessening both extremes on land.

Moderation need not imply monotony. Situated as it is between Asia and the ocean, between the sub-tropics and the North Pole, Europe is an atmospheric battlefield. In winter Eastern Europe, unwarmed by sea, becomes a centre of cold, heavy air, building up a zone of high pressure from which bitter east and polar winds sweep across western Europe. In the summer, the opposite happens: the land grows hot, the warm air rises, and lower pressure sucks in the cooler, damp west wind. At the same time, there are north-south seasonal movements. The high-pressure area over the Azores and the Sahara shifts with the tilt of the earth *vis-à-vis* the sun, moving north in summer to make southern Europe a tourist playground, and in winter going south to leave the Mediterranean cooler, although still sheltered by the Alps from the chillier rains of the north-west. With spring and autumn as transitional phases, western Europe in particular has the traditional four seasons. In world terms, this is no norm, but an exception – although European literature has exported the concept, with all its emotive overtones, to climates where much of Shelley, Wordsworth, and James Thomson makes little sense.

Underlying and complicating these seasonal movements is the general west-east drift of Atlantic whirlwinds from the regions of Iceland and Newfoundland. Here, polar and tropical air-masses meet, clash, and spin, then are carried eastward by the earth's rotation, bringing to western Europe its characteristically chancy and unsettled weather. As the French humorist Pierre Daninos once put it,

If you listen to the French meteorological bulletins, the bad weather is always coming from elsewhere—so much so that if elsewhere did not exist, the weather would always be perfectly good over France. "Depression from Iceland, anti-cyclone from the Azores, cold currents from the Shetlands, rainy spells from Scotland...." It's always these damned foreigners.

Even the "bad weather", however changeable, is moderate. Only on a few exposed north-western slopes in Scotland, southern Norway, and the Alps, is the annual rainfall more than eighty inches, compared with well over 100 in parts of West Africa and much of Asia, including 425 at Cherrapunji in Assam, possibly the rainiest spot on earth. Over most of Europe, the year's rainfall is between twenty and forty inches – about the same as in Chicago, and rather less than in New York.

Yet, for all its moderation, Europe is also varied. The sea itself is partly responsible, separating land-masses, and isolating peninsulas like southern Italy or islands like Great Britain. What makes one people, like the Belgians, predominantly landlubbers, while their neighbours the Dutch become seafarers, remains a mystery; but Europe's seas and rivers have certainly helped differentiate some of her inhabitants even as they have linked others. Those Europeans who became the world's great navigators – Dutch, British, Italian, Spanish, Portuguese, north German, Breton, Norwegian – may have shared the camaraderie of the sea, but they also shared its rivalry; and they still differ notably from the inhabitants of the hinterland, especially to the east. Joseph Conrad was an exceptional Pole.

But the mountains are what chiefly account for Europe's diversity. In earlier times, they restricted the movement of people, isolating some hardy communities, strengthening independence and individuality. Even today, when human travel is so much easier and faster, the mountain ranges still act as

The Europeans

climatic barriers. Broadly, they have divided Europe into four characteristic areas: the old, hard mountains of the north and north-west; the great central plain opening eastwards; the broken Hercynian belt from the Channel to the Black Sea; and the high young mountain ranges on the shores of the Mediterranean. Each has its own climate, soil, and vegetation: each has made its own contribution to Europe's wealth.

To the north, in much of Russia and Scandinavia, there are very short hot summers – familiar in Ingmar Bergman's films – and the rest of the year is very cold. In the extreme north, on the tundra, the main natural growth is moss, thick lichen (including the so-called "reindeer moss"), and low bushes of dwarf willow and birch; but the long days of the short summer also produce a number of lush Nordic meadows. The rest of the north is a forest region. Here, below a dark surface, the subsoil tends to be an ashlike *podsol* from which the mineral salts have been leached and washed downwards, forming a solid layer underneath. Its characteristic products are the Norway spruce and Scots pine, intermingled with silver birch, all of which originally settled there some 8,000 to 5,000 years ago, after the latest ice age.

Europe's central belt has cold winters and hot summers. To the east, the extremes grow greater; fewer trees take root here except near rivers, and the typical natural lands are rolling grassy steppes, merging into desert further south. To the west, in more maritime regions, rain falls all the year round; winters are warmer, and summers less hot. Here, most of the soil is finer, darker, richer, and damper, riddled by earthworms and composted with leaf-mould from the deciduous forests of oak, elm, linden, and alder that followed the northern conifers and were later joined by beech from the Danube basin. Where the forest are cleared, they tend to be replaced by meadowland; here and there, in sandy or rocky areas, there has probably always been moorland and heath.

The Mediterranean, finally, has warm, wet winters and hot dry summers. Its soil is often poor, then red limestone, and its typical native plants are woody dry evergreens – olive, holm-oak, cork-oak, Lebanese cedar, or the Aleppo pine, whose needle-like leaves resist the parching effects of the sun just as those of the northern conifers resist the cold. In the hottest and dryest southern areas there is also a *maquis* of thorny bushes and scrub.

A blind man might recognize each of these areas by feel and smell alone: the bitter cold and crunchy moss of the tundra; the brisk forest air of Scandinavia; the winds blowing across the Russian steppes; the gentle, dewy, earthy atmosphere of western Europe, especially after rain; the rock and brushwood underfoot around the Mediterranean, with its dry, resinous, peppery air, its sweet wild-flower scents in early spring, and in winter the smell of oak and olive-wood burning.

And yet, especially in the west, he might well be mistaken. It was the Russian Imperial Bureau of Soils that in the late nineteenth century first divided the map of Europe's soil into these climatic regions; and although partly confirmed by later studies, the classification clearly makes more sense on the flat expanses of central and eastern Europe than among the complex corrugations of the west. Here, in fact, the multiplicity of Europe's soil and vegetation is greatest of all. In the north, as on the highest Alps, *podsols* cover the older rock; but elsewhere there is immense diversity: peat-bogs, glacial "boulder clay", light sandy soil, loess and rich loam over limestone hills, alluvial deposits in the valleys, and clays formed chiefly from weathered granite on some of the plateaux. Leaching and weathering, so typical of the northern and mountainous *podsols*, is less extensive in southern and western Europe, partly owing to the more general humidity – fog, dew, and continual drizzle rather than storms and cloudbursts. Even the obelisk in the Place de la Concorde in Paris has weathered less in Europe's mild, damp climate than its slightly smaller counterpart in Central Park, New York. The Mediterranean basin, finally, is not made up merely of meagre limestone: it contains fertile acres of many other soils, some of them on the still dangerous slopes of Vesuvius and Etna –

which D. H. Lawrence called "that wicked witch, resting her thick white snow under heaven, and slowly, slowly rolling her orange-coloured smoke."

Every so often, even now, the witch spills out her lava. A slow tide of destruction pours downhill, and television viewers in the rest of Europe see peasants pack up their belongings, priests invoke divine providence, and villages engulfed or spared. But after each disaster – or miracle – the villagers go back: the lava tide means death, but its ash brings life and fertility. Man has learned to live with Etna, and on it – whatever the price. So doing, he has made a home for himself – cutting back oak-trees, terracing the slopes, walling off groves of fruit-trees. All over Europe, indeed, man's long struggle with nature has radically changed the landscape, soil, and vegetation left by the far longer ages of geological and prehistoric time.

Were it not for man, most of Europe would still be covered by forest, as nearly three-quarters of Finland and over half of Sweden and Russia still are. Elsewhere, the proportion now varies between forty per cent in Austria and only seven in the British Isles. Not for nothing do fairy-tales feature woodcutters.

But man is also a planter. To preserve the soil from erosion after the forests were felled, he not only built stepped terraces: he learned to replace some of the trees, as in the *rideaux* or "screens" that shield the chalky slopes of Picardy. He found that livestock, as well as lava, could manure the land; and he learned to irrigate. Among the rocks of Malta today, fitted to metal drainpipes with windmills imported from America, there are still many narrow stone aqueducts, some of which may date from pre-Roman times. With care and sweat, in other words, not only the land that fed and was fed by the deciduous forests, but also more barren stretches, could gradually be made rich.

Today, nevertheless, Europe's crops and livestock still reflect the diversity of her climate and soil. Oats, for instance, flourish in the north – in Scotland, Denmark, southern Norway and Finland, and much of Russia, as well as in northern France and Bohemia. Sheep predominate in some of the same areas, notably the British Isles. Rye does well in the poorish soil of northern central Europe: hence the popularity of rye bread in Germany, Poland, and Russia – as in America, the home of so many refugees. The Low Countries, Germany, and Poland are also the chief producers and consumers of potatoes and pigs. Winter wheat is grown in the richer lands of East Anglia, northern and western France, the Rhône valley, parts of Spain, Italy, and the Balkans, as well as on the Russian steppes, which are also a great source of spring wheat. Slightly moister parts of this same broad belt, especially to the west, make good pasture for cattle. Around the Mediterranean, the less arid areas produce maize, while rockier, hotter regions grow oranges, lemons, olives, and grapes. In these latitudes, too, as on Europe's more barren uplands, there are many more sheep and goats. Here and there, finally, cultural freaks occur. Belgium, perhaps as a result of the Spanish occupation, grows expensive grapes, advertised to the passing motorist as "foodful and healing". Malta, for many years a British naval base, still grows cabbages and cauliflowers, and boasts the only Marks and Spencer's in the Mediterranean.

Europe's riches are also partly mineral. Coal is the most extensive, scattered across the great central belt of Europe from Great Britain, northern France and Belgium, the Campine, the Ruhr, and the Saar, to Upper Silesia and the Tula and Donets coalfields of the USSR. Power comes also from Europe's many water-courses, especially in Scandinavia and the various mountains of the Alpine system. The mountains, again, provide the high-grade iron ore found in Spain and Sweden, although ore of lower quality occurs in the central belt from Cleveland and the Midlands in Britain to Lorraine, Luxembourg, and Belgium. North Germany has some lead, zinc, and copper, as does southern Spain; Cornwall used to have tin; and there are smaller deposits of these and other minerals elsewhere. Oil, finally, is found mainly in Rumania and Russia, while natural gas has been tapped in various

23

places, including France, Italy, Germany, the Netherlands, and the North Sea.

Many of these resources were discovered and exploited late in Europe's history; and even now they are meagre compared with those of other continents. Clearly, her original wealth was due in large part to her climate and vegetation. As the geographer Strabo wrote in the first century BC,

> this part of the world is the most varied; ... owing to its climate it is the most favourable to industry and civilization.... But its chief advantage is this: that of all the foodstuffs necessary to life, Europe produces the best.... In addition, it has abundant cattle and few wild beasts.

A climate uniquely favourable, self-sufficiency in agriculture, superior food: many since Strabo have claimed these virtues for their country or their continent – although latterly lamenting, not celebrating, the shortage of wild beasts. Nearly 2,000 years after Strabo, Jean-Jacques Rousseau gave another reason for Europe's prosperity. By comparison with other continents, he argued, Europe was not only "more generally fertile", but also "better linked in all its parts", chiefly by "the multitude of rivers that flow in different directions, making communications easy."

Indeed, although the mountains that span Europe have made for diversity, they have never completely prevented travel. The rivers that flow from them – the Loire, the Garonne, the Seine, the Po, the Rhine, the Danube, the Weser, the Elbe, the Oder, the Vistula, the Dvinas, the Don, the Dnieper, the Volga – many of them broad and slow, with few falls and rapids, few of them freezing in winter, form with their tributaries a tassel of routes across the continent. Only the Pyrenees and the Caucasus remain really formidable barriers. The Scandinavian mountains have steep spinal ranges, but are otherwise flattened. The Hercynian range is reduced to massifs; and even the Alps are threaded by valleys with passes in between. Finally, where land travel is hardest, in the

Mediterranean peninsulas, the warm, tideless, and fairly predictable sea is a permanent potential highway.

Rousseau, however, added a further explanation for Europe's close-knit wealth: "the restlessness of its inhabitants, which leads them to travel incessantly and move from one country to another." "Europe," he concluded, "is not only — like Asia or Africa — an imaginary collection of peoples with nothing in common but a name. It is a real society."

Man's incessant handiwork has already been glimpsed in the making of the European landscape. The time has come to people that landscape, and to look more closely at the origins and development of European man.

3

The Melting-Pot

Man is a Tool-using Animal.... Weak in himself, and of
small stature, he stands on a basis, at most for the flattest-
soled, of some half-square foot, insecurely enough; he has
to straddle out his legs, lest the very wind supplant him.
Feeblest of bipeds! Three quintals are a crushing load for
him; the steer of the meadow tosses him aloft, like a waste
rag. Nevertheless he can use Tools, can devise Tools: with
these the granite mountain melts into light dust before him;
he kneads glowing iron, as if it were soft paste; seas are his
smooth highway, winds and fire his unwearying steeds. Nowhere do you find him without Tools; without Tools he is
nothing, with Tools he is all.

THOMAS CARLYLE, *Sartor Resartus*

MAN owes his nature to his weakness. His remotest
ancestors seem to have lived some twenty million years
ago in south-east Africa. Most of their lives they spent in the
trees, fairly safe from the predators that stalked them. They
probably fed on fruit within reach, although they seem also
to have come down to drink – and sometimes to be killed.
Then, some millions of years later, the climate altered. Very
slowly, the land dried up. The trees gradually died; and what
had once been jungle or forest turned into open savannah, like
much of Africa today. The dwindling groves became crowded

and were fought for: the strong displaced the weak. Those who remained in the trees became the probable ancestors of the later great apes. The weaklings who were forced to the ground eventually gave rise to man.

Already they had some features that equipped them for their new life. Their eyes were set in the front of their heads, depriving them of all-round vision, but enabling them to see stereoscopically, with accurate judgement of distance and space. Their forepaws had already become capable of a hook-like grasp: on the ground, with defter fingers and, increasingly, thumbs, they turned into a form of forceps. In the trees, their bodies had grown used to being upright as well as horizontal, and their hearts had strengthened to pump blood upward for the brain. Now, amid the tall grasses, they learned to stand.

Life was dangerous on the ground, and natural selection proceeded faster. Those who survived had firm feet, strong legs, and quick wits. They no longer needed apelike arms to swing or walk with; their hands were free to pick up and carry as well as to grasp. Food was scarcer, so they had to experiment – with grubs, eggs, small reptiles, and carrion left by the predators. They also began to hunt.

Small young animals, or those weakened by disease and ageing, were easy prey; but others could only be overcome by organization and weapons. To hunt in groups meant planning and communication, by cries as well as gestures. To obtain effective weapons meant not only collecting what lay to hand in the form of stones, branches, and the bones of animals, but also laboriously shaping them into spears, clubs, and crude blades.

Several non-human animals use rudimentary tools or weapons: men themselves retain pre-human features, such as the large roots of their canine teeth. If today the distinctions between monkeys, apes, and men are firm and manifest, this was not always so. The so-called "missing link" was not one, but many. Several types of primate emerged from the common ancestral stock before the first identifiable men. Long ago, the ancestors of today's monkeys diverged from it; then, between ten and five million years ago, the great apes; then, about two million years ago, the australopithecines. Their remains have been found in Java as well as in Africa. Like man, they walked erect, ate meat, and made stone weapons; but they had larger jaws and smaller brains. At length, they died out. The next to emerge, between a million and five hundred thousand years ago, were the pithecanthropines, called by some *Homo erectus* in token of their clear kinship with modern man. As the name implies, they stood upright: they were five to five foot six inches tall. Their teeth and jaws were still evolving; and the size of their brain-case varied from 900 to 1,250 cubic centimetres, as against some 700 for the australopithecines and 1,100 to 1,700 for *Homo sapiens sapiens*. Some of them, in other words, may well have had bigger brains than some men living today. They made right-handed stone implements, including choppers and scrapers; they ate meat, especially venison and perhaps each other; they used fire and probably some form of language.

Remains with pithecanthropine characteristics have been found in sites as various as Morocco and Algeria, eastern and southern Africa, Java, Pekin, and southern China. Whether they formed one family is doubtful; where the different branches came from is a mystery; but some of them were very probably among the first Europeans.

It was in 1960, in a grotto in Provence, that two French investigators made the crucial discovery. In the Escale cave at St-Estève-Janson in the valley of the Durance in the Bouches-du-Rhône *département*, Eugène and Marie-Françoise Bonifay found large numbers of bones belonging to extinct animals, together with a few fragmentary limestone tools. Prehistoric hunters had lived and eaten there. More important, the rock was cracked and reddened in at least five places, some a yard wide, with vestiges of ash and charcoal. The hunters had lit fires: they had been men. The date of the site was probably some 750,000 years ago – within the age of the pithecanthropines. No human remains have yet been found there; but for the present the Escale cave looks very like the earliest known home of European men.

How did they get there? If, as seems likely, they were pithecanthropines whose ancestors came from Africa, they could have come up through Spain. At that time, the Mediterranean may well have been spanned by several land-bridges – across the Straits of Gibraltar, from Tunisia to Sicily and Italy, and across the Turkish straits at either end of the Sea of Marmara. Some believe that the Biblical Flood was a tidal wave caused when an earthquake cracked the bridges. At all events, Spain also bears traces of very early man. A few years after the Escale cave discovery, the American scholar F. Clark Howell unearthed hand-axes and charred wood at Torralba and Ambrona – the only traces left, some 300,000 years ago, by elephant hunters who seem to have used fire to drive their quarry into a swamp or perhaps a man-made pit.

The earliest human bone found in Europe dates from between the Escale and the Torralba vestiges, about 500,000 years ago. This is a lower jaw found near Heidelberg in 1907 – the so-called "Mauer mandible". Its owner was probably a hunter of rhinoceros and elephant, whose bones were found nearby. He may possibly have been a pithecanthropine: but his jaw was large and his chin receding – both more primitive features; while his teeth were small and advanced. Rather later than the Heidelberg fragment are parts of a skull and some teeth discovered at Vértesszöllös, near Budapest, in 1965. Animal bones found with it suggest that it dates from about 400,000 years ago. Although thick, and similar in some respects to pithecanthropine remains, the Vértesszöllös skull is more rounded and has a larger brain capacity – about 1,400 cubic centimetres, or just below the average for modern man. Both Heidelberg man and Vértesszöllös man, that is, were possibly intermediate between the pithecanthropines – *Homo erectus* – and *Homo sapiens*. They may have evolved from pithecanthropines who had entered Europe through Spain; or their ancestors, whether pithecanthropine or not, may have come from further east. Nor is there any proof that today's

Europeans are among their descendants. For the present, they are merely fragmentary milestones in the slow and halting evolution of man.

Closer to *Homo sapiens* are further remains in Britain, Germany, and France. At Swanscombe, south of the Thames between Dartford and Gravesend, parts of a woman's skull have been found, with animal bones and stone tools that date from about 250,000 years ago. About 50,000 years younger is a complete skull, probably that of a murdered woman, found near Steinheim in Germany. Slightly later is a lower jaw discovered in a cave at Montmaurin in the French Pyrenees. All three show mixed features. The Swanscombe fragment is thick, but it probably formed part of a sizeable brain-case; the Steinheim skull is small, low-vaulted, and heavy-browed, but it has a rounded back and a forehead less sloping than in *Homo erectus;* the Montmaurin mandible is chinless and broad, like that from Heidelberg, but rather smaller. All in fact appear to be intermediate precursors of later man.

Still more significant are two rather younger skull fragments unearthed in 1947 at Fontéchevade, to the west of Angoulême in the Charente. Although thick, these have small brow ridges and a large brain capacity – about 1,450 cubic centimetres: both are thus very similar to those of modern man. The flint tools found with them date from between 120,000 and 200,000 years ago. Taken together, therefore, the Fontéchevade finds suggest that representatives of *Homo sapiens,* looking much like modern men, were living in Europe long before the fourth and latest major ice age. They may well have been the remote ancestors of some present-day Europeans.

Between then and now, however, stands not only an interval of many thousands of years, but also the enigmatic figure of Neandertal man.

He owes his title to an almost forgotten German hymn-writer, Joachim Neumann, who used "Neander" – the Greek form of his surname – as a pseudonym, and had a valley or *Tal* named after him. In 1887, in a limestone cave in that valley, which is really a deep ravine on the Düssel, near Düsseldorf, an almost complete skeleton of a prehistoric man was unearthed. Similar finds have since been made at La Chapelle-aux-Saints in the Corrèze, at Moustier and La Fer-rassie in the nearby Dordogne, and at various sites in Italy, Greece, and elsewhere, as well as in Africa and Asia. Their dates range roughly from 125,000 to 70,000 years ago.

In some cases, at least, Neandertal man was a tough-looking figure – heavily built and stocky, about five feet tall, with a rugged, low-vaulted skull, a sloping forehead, beetling brows, a broad nose, a massive jaw, a receding chin, and large teeth. For this reason, it was long believed that he was an evolu-tionary throwback. It was assumed that he had come and then vanished, quite quickly supplanted by men closer in time and type to *Homo sapiens*. Perhaps it was reassuring to feel that so hulking a creature had no place in modern Europe's ances-tral stock.

This now seems less certain. Indeed, Neandertal man was far from being the brute of popular legend. Originally, he was thought to have had a bowed posture and a shambling gait: he is now known to have suffered from arthritis. Normally, he stood fairly upright, and his feet were very like our own. His brain was large, between 1,300 and 1,650 cubic centimetres – high in the upper range for modern man. He hunted big game, including bears and mammoths, with the aid of pit-traps; in the colder periods he probably wore animal skins for warmth. As some remains show, he was capable of caring for the sick and crippled; and he buried his dead. He pillowed their heads and protected them with stone slabs, in one case roughly carved; he folded their legs against their bodies, and sometimes care-fully surrounded them with animal bones or white stones. In a grave only recently discovered, the dead man had been laid on pine boughs strewn with wild flowers.

Nor, finally, were all Neandertal men and women as ugly as their traditional stereotype. It seems likely, indeed, that natural selection during the ice age favoured the thicker build of those in colder areas. Others were slightly more lissom. In the caves on Mount Carmel, for instance, several skeletons have been found with both modern and Neandertal features: sometimes one predominates, sometimes the other. Since *Homo sapiens* was already about at the time, it seems very possible that Neandertal man was not simply supplanted, but may actually have interbred. Already before the end of the ice ages, in other words, Europe may have begun to be a melting-pot of peoples.

From now on they appeared with increasing speed. Some 50,000 years ago, possibly through the Balkans from Asia, came the earliest of those to be known later as Cro-Magnon man. Nearly six feet tall, with a thin skull, a high forehead, a small brow ridge, a broad face, a high-bridged nose, square jaw, jutting chin, and small teeth, he was a strapping and presentable forefather for later generations. In one case at least, his brain capacity was about 1,590 cubic centimetres. A contemporary portrait – a bas-relief at Angles-sur-Anglin east of Poitiers – shows a pale, wide-eyed face with a prominent nose, prim lips, and black hair and beard. The site from which he takes his name was near Les Eyzies in the rich, green, winding valley of the Vézère in the Dordogne *département* – still one of the most beautiful and gastronomically rewarding areas of France. Sheltered and well watered, with extensive caves in its steep limestone cliffs and no doubt abundant game on its pastures, the valley has attracted many later visitors and settlers, including mediaeval men who used some of its overhanging rock-shelters as niches for their own houses.

Cro-Magnon man was by no means isolated. In the shelter where his bones were found, there were not only the remains of bison, elephants, horses, mammoth, and reindeer, but also a number of sea-shells – although the nearest coastline was at least 100 miles away. Clearly there was much travel, and perhaps even trade. Vestiges of men from this same broad epoch – between 30,000 and 15,000 years ago – have been found at Combe Capelle and Chancelade in Périgord, at Aurignac in the lower Pyrenees, in the Grimaldi caves between Monaco and the Italian Riviera, at Obercassel in Germany, at Brünn and Předmost in Czechoslovakia, and even as far north as the Paviland cave in Wales.

Several of these finds show hybrid features: in Combe Capelle and Czechoslovakia, an apparent mixture of *Homo sapiens* and Neandertal man; in the Grimaldi caves a possible negroid strain, perhaps from Africa; at Chancelade and Obercassel, a broad jaw and Eskimo-like cheekbones – seen also in the small, charming ivory head of a girl found at Brassempouy in south-western France. If appearances can be trusted, Europeans were already of mongrel stock in the age of Cro-Magnon man.

Equally mixed and changing were their tools, weapons, and works of art, painstakingly classified by archaeologists into techniques and styles that inevitably merged and overlapped, lapsed and reappeared, were communicated, pooled, and copied. Sometimes, a culture can be identified with a people; but in most cases it can only be known by its products. To speak of the Levalloisians, the Acheulians, the Mousterians, the Périgordians, the Châtelperronians, the Gravettians, the Aurignacians, the Solutreans, the Magdalenians, the Azilians, the Sauveterrians, or the Tardenoisians, is simply to use a convenient shorthand for the group or groups whose artifacts are of the types named after these various sites. Yet, as time went by, there were many technical changes. New ways of shaping stone were developed; more effective tools and weapons were devised; new demands – for needles, spoons, or necklaces – produced new materials and implements, or new ways of making them; with growing skill, carving became more decorative and representational; eventually, cave painting began.

It is this, the best known of it at Lascaux, about fifteen miles upstream from Les Eyzies, that gives the most vivid picture of how the Europeans then lived. Lascaux was probably frequented for about a thousand years, around 15,000 years ago. At that time, as in the preceding period, most of Europe was still cold. The ice ages were ending, but gradually and with later fluctuations: a final chilly half-millennium occurred between 10,800 and 10,300 years ago. In the colder phases, much of the land was part-tundra, part-steppe, and the trees were mainly dwarf varieties. Many of the animals were thick-coated, woolly creatures – bison, musk-ox, bear, and mammoth; others included wild horses, reindeer, and arctic hare. Men lived chiefly by hunting them, with spears, arrows, sinew-snares, and pit-traps; at Solutré near Mâcon in Burgundy, they herded wild horses to their deaths over a rocky cliff. Those who lived near rivers, lakes, or sea-shores caught fish, with harpoons, flint hooks, and wicker traps; they also collected oysters, and like their inland cousins ate berries and nuts. In places, they settled – perhaps less often in caves than in rock-shelters; when they moved on in search of game, some of them used tents made from animal hide. Hides were also their clothing, and both men and women wore necklaces, pendants, and bracelets made from bone, horn, and shells. Families, perhaps polygamous, formed tribes guided by shamans and served by skilful artisans and artists. They may have practised magic, to bring fertility and speed the hunt; they certainly danced, sometimes in animal masks and skins. Like Neandertal man, they buried their dead ceremoniously. Some, perhaps outlaws, seem still to have been cannibals. Some had missing or truncated fingers, shown by hand-prints on the walls of caves; but whether this was due to accident, punishment, or ritual mutilation remains unknown.

Climatic changes brought this way of life to an end. In Europe, although still gradual, they were relatively rapid. As the continent grew warmer, its vegetation altered. Some 10,300 years ago, true birch and willow began to replace their dwarf varieties; later came pine and hazel, and finally the full deciduous forests. Red- and roe-deer, aurochs, elk, and wild pigs were soon to appear in them; but the older and bigger arctic game was vanishing, some of it exterminated by man's over-efficient technology, some starved of its grazing, some – like the reindeer – roaming further north. Short of food, and of the raw materials provided by mammoth tusks and reindeer antlers, man and his art grew poorer. He now had to seek smaller prey or move northward too, pushing further into Scandinavia and Britain. And as the northern ice retreated, new obstacles replaced it. About 9,000 years ago, the melting glaciers flooded the southern part of what is now the North Sea, which until then had been dry: Britain was now an island. Men adapted quickly enough to a maritime existence. Boats of a sort – perhaps a form of kayak – were not new at this time; but the earliest remains of them so far discovered are a wooden paddle at Star Carr in north-east England, dating from about 9,000 years ago, and a dugout canoe found at Pesse in Holland, which is about 8,400 years old.

Europe was not the only area to undergo climatic changes. Something similar had already happened in Asia Minor, to the south-east. Turkey, Syria, Jordan, Iraq, and the northern part of Saudi Arabia began to experience warmer weather about 10,000 years ago; and farming began to flourish there at least two millennia before its full development in Europe.

The traditional picture of this crucial transformation is temptingly simple. Agriculture, it was thought, began in the Middle East because the sun had parched the pastures and driven the game away. Deprived of meat, men began eating grain. At first, it had grown wild; then it was sown deliberately. This necessitated semi-permanent settlements – the beginning of village life. Dogs had already been used for hunting; now they became man's first domestic animal. With a settled life, technology improved rapidly: stonework became sophisticated; pottery developed; metalwork began. Villages became towns, then rich cities, where writing was invented about 5,000 years ago. As the warmer weather spread north and westwards, men followed in search of land and raw materials, especially the copper and tin ores that were needed to make bronze. Gradually, they colonized Europe through Minoan Crete and Mycenaean Greece, taking their culture with them: the vast stone monuments of western Europe, at Carnac, Stonehenge, and elsewhere, were the product of skills imported from the eastern Mediterranean, as were Europe's metallurgy and her weapons of war. The cradle of civilization, for both good and evil, was the Near and Middle East, the home of the sun and the pyramids.

Much of this general picture may be valid; but almost every detail is wrong. On a world scale, the Middle East was not the only source of farming: it began independently in the Americas and especially in Mexico, as perhaps elsewhere. Parched soil would indeed have driven game away, but Asia Minor at that time was no desert: enjoying both warmth and rain, it was a fairly fertile land of valleys, springs, and streams. The earliest plantings were made not only for food, but for a variety of purposes – for protection, in the case of thorn bushes, or for dyes, drugs, gourds, and ornaments. It was not farming that led to the first settlements: at Tell Murebat in Syria near the Euphrates, there was a village 9,500 years ago whose inhabitants lived by hunting, although they also ate wild grain. Similar, earlier settlements have been found in Europe. Dogs, although intelligent, were not necessarily used as hunting companions; before they became pets or servants, they were also prey. Nor were they the first domestic animals. Already, in Europe, men may have tamed reindeer; at Zawi Chemi Shanidar in Iraq, 11,000 years ago, they had domesticated sheep.

The stonemasons of the eastern Mediterranean were certainly impressive; but corrected radio-carbon dating suggests that here too traditional notions need to be revised. Some of the passage graves in France now seem to have predated collective burial in the Aegean; Ggantija and other "temples" in the Maltese islands, as well as Los Millares in Spain and New Grange in Ireland, appear to have been built more than 5,000 years ago – before the first settlers in eastern Crete and long before the first Egyptian pyramid. Even Stonehenge was probably begun, it now seems, some 4,000 years ago, before the great palaces of Knossos, Phaistos, and Mallia in Minoan Crete. Metallurgy of at least a primitive kind is admittedly first detectable in Asia Minor: a beaten copper pendant from about 10,500 years ago has been found at Shanidar, and copper pins from 9,000 years ago at Diyarbakir in Turkey. But the first trace of metal-work in conjunction with pottery kilns capable of smelting ore comes from the Balkans of more than 6,000 years ago, in the so-called Gumelnitsa culture of Bulgaria and Rumania. Even writing, finally, may not have originated only in the Middle East. A grave pit in Rumania excavated in 1967 yielded three baked tablets of local clay with what look like written characters incised in them; the date provisionally ascribed to them, again, is more than 6,000 years ago.

Men almost always underrate their own predecessors. Owing to the oddities of much mediaeval draughtsmanship, we tend to picture mediaeval man as a clownish, stunted simpleton, with an adenoidal goggle and tadpole's limbs contorted to fit the lack of space and perspective. Much further back, Neandertal man used to seem a clumsy, shambling ape-man. Even Cro-Magnon man, whose cousins or close descendants produced delicately graceful engravings and the noble, spirited beasts of the Lascaux cave-paintings, is abominably libelled by the statue erected to him above his own home at Les Eyzies: a hulking yeti with his head sunk in his shoulders, as if trying to heave his way out of the primeval rock – no doubt to get at his creator, the French sculptor Dardé. Modern man, thrust back into a Cro-Magnon environment, would find life difficult, even with memories of later technology to help him; without them, many would be baffled, uninventive, and soon dead. As it was, the man of those ages had to invent continually: life was a test of ingenuity as well as strength. As climate and vegetation changed, the price of survival was eternal vigilance – not only against danger, but also in search of new foods, new materials, and new skills. Natural selection favoured wide-awake intelligence. So it should be no surprise to find that some discoveries may have been made, and some new methods originated, in Europe as well as in Asia Minor. Necessity is the mother of invention wherever the context is right.

What is certain is that traffic between the two continents now developed very rapidly. This too was only natural, since the conventional dividing-line between them meant even less then than it does today. The Turkish straits were very narrow; there were passes through and routes round the Caucasus mountains; the land to the north was one rolling expanse of forest and steppe. There was little to stop mixed farming peoples gradually following their sheep and goat flocks into Europe; and there is much evidence to suggest that they did. To this extent Europe's agriculture was indeed largely the offspring of the eastern Mediterranean; on land, the traffic was mainly one-way.

But a second set of routes – the sea-routes – linked Europe with Asia Minor; and here the sequence is less clear-cut. Many of Europe's great stone monuments are found near the coast, if not on it – in Malta and Gozo; in eastern Sicily, Sardinia, and southern Italy; at Fontvielle in Provence, between Arles and Les Baux; at Los Millares in southern Spain, and at Alcalá and Palmella in Portugal; at Carnac in Brittany; at New Grange in Ireland; at Maes Howe in the Orkneys; and in Denmark, southern Sweden, north Germany, and northern Holland. Technical resemblances suggest that many of these are interrelated; and stylistic similarities in some of the later carvings on them make it likely that the links persisted for many years. Much more doubtful are the origins of this megalithic culture. Revised carbon dating seems now to rule out Minoan Crete; Malta is a possibility, although small and isolated; the Iberian peninsula might seem a better candidate, except that its megaliths appear to be later than some of those in France. Could it be that the movement took place not from the eastern Mediterranean to western Europe, but the other way? This too would contradict some of the evidence. A further and perhaps more plausible theory is that megalithic tombs may have begun to be built independently at several separate places; another, that their builders moved in different directions at various times. What led them to travel? Missionary zeal? Curiosity? A search for living space, for mineral ores, for markets? What motives made the British Empire or sent men to the moon?

Whatever answers may one day be given, the megaliths are still gigantic question-marks. What is clear is the skill of the men who transported and erected them; what is even more impressive is the intellectual capacity of their architects. In the case of the megalithic tombs, their purpose can be described as religious; but religion alone may not explain the stone alignments at Carnac or the concentric rings at Stonehenge. Perhaps here, as in many communities, it was mingled with early science. Recent calculations have shown that both Stonehenge and Carnac are extremely accurate celestial calendars. This too is not unnatural. Close observation of the sky is to be expected in sea-faring peoples who at times sailed out of sight of land.

Sea and land routes alike saw much traffic in the millennia and the centuries that followed. By this time Europe was in two senses a genuine melting-pot.

In the first and literal sense, it was from now on that metalwork – first in copper and bronze, then later in iron – spread throughout the continent, developing far more quickly than it had in the Middle East. In the second sense, these and other contemporary skills, including pottery and house-building, seem to have been conveyed by some of the huge variety of peoples who were now stirred into the cauldron of Europe's ancestral stock.

Altogether, more than thirty such peoples – many more, if sub-groups are counted – make up the ancestry of Europeans today. Some had recognizable genetic features; others were represented by a culture or a language. Some were indigenous; others were newcomers, many of them warlike invaders. Most were assimilated; a few remained more or less aloof as a ruling aristocracy; some, especially in later centuries, were largely repulsed.

First came the influx of farmers. One early group entered Thessaly; another spread through the Balkans, fanning out into Hungary and the Ukraine. The stocky "Danubians" left their mark on Europe from Russia to the Low Countries, clearing the forests to plant barley, beans, flax, and wheat.

Another group, coming by sea along the Mediterranean coast, brought shell-decorated pottery; further west, stockbreeders settled round Spain and Portugal and the south of France before moving up the Rhône valley and eventually into Brittany and the British Isles.

Then came warriors and traders. The first to arrive in large numbers were the "Battle-axe People" – tall, strongly-built horsemen from the Russian steppes, who seem to have introduced copper-working into much of Europe. It was from Spain rather than the east, however, that copper technology spread most widely – not merely because Spain was a rich source of ore, but also because it was almost certainly the home of the so-called "Beaker Folk". This, like so many similar titles, is misleading. To the unwary, it might suggest a mild freemasonry of tall, eager, inquiring figures, stalking quickly across Europe on bird-like legs. In fact, it denotes a culture, named on account of its bell-shaped pottery drinking-mugs, probably used for beer. Those of its representatives who entered Britain were large and robust, with big round skulls. Beginning well over 4,000 years ago, they had roamed over most of western Europe from Spain to the Balkans and the Baltic before turning back to reach the western coasts again within about 500 years. As well-armed traders and tinkers, they taught and learned from the tribes they encountered; they also no doubt interbred with them, adding once more to Europe's ethnic mixture.

Other traders arrived by sea. The Phoenicians, dark-skinned as their name implies, either by nature or from exposure, came from Syria and Palestine over 3,000 years ago, working their way along the Mediterranean and Atlantic coasts. A few hundred years later, in the tenth, ninth, and eighth centuries BC, the Etruscans moved from Asia Minor into Italy, where they were gradually absorbed into the population – although hill-towns like Volterra in Tuscany still have many relics of their enigmatic presence, largely in the calm reclining figures carved on their cinerary urns.

By this time the whole of Europe was criss-crossed by trade-

routes. Perhaps the best attested are those whereby amber –
fossilized pine resin – from the North Sea and the Baltic was
brought south to the Adriatic in exchange for bronze. But
there were many others. The result was great cultural confusion – and headaches for later archaeologists. Throughout
the continent and its islands, objects and styles began to appear very far from their places of origin. Mediterranean
motifs were copied in Norway and Sweden; Greek artifacts
turned up in Britain; products from northern Europe were
prized in Italy and the Balkans. Internal migration stirred the
cauldron even more. In the thirteenth century BC, for instance, a new form of burial had begun to spread from the
northern Balkans to Italy, Poland, Germany, and eastern
France. Three centuries later, it reached north-west Europe
and Spain. Those responsible have been variously identified
as Germans, Slavs, or even Illyrians. Again, from the ninth
century BC onwards, iron-workers from around Halstatt in
Austria, whose trade had ultimately derived from the Hittites
of Asia Minor, began to penetrate Italy and the Balkans; they
also passed their skill to the upper Rhineland Celts in the
north-west. Ethnically, the Celts were already a mixture, perhaps descended from both the "Battle-axe People" and the
"Beaker Folk". Some 400 years later, they too began to multiply and grow footloose. They came down through the Alps
into Italy, where they sacked Rome in 390 BC; they moved
into the Balkans and Greece, and even east as far as Asia
Minor; they went westward into Belgium, France, and Britain,
where some of them were still arriving when the Romans
came.

Rome, of course, left its stamp on the whole of Europe; but
unlike most of their predecessors, the Romans themselves –
the original Italici – were colonists rather than immigrants.
Like the British in India, they staffed their Empire without
peopling it: they left more monuments than sons. More important in this respect were the "barbarian" invaders who
broke through the Empire's defences. Among the first were the
ferocious Scythians, from Sarmatia to the north and east; but

41

by far the most numerous were the teeming tribes of the Goths.

Gothic pirates and land marauders had already probed southwards before the time of Christ; but the great expansion covered the next five centuries. In the third century AD, the Goths established eastern and western confederacies – of the Ostrogoths and Visigoths – in the area of the Black Sea. Over the following 200 years, the Visigoths drove their way into the Roman Empire, eventually attacking Rome itself and setting up kingdoms as far west as France and Spain. In the end, they were driven out by the Franks – themselves a Gothonic-speaking people – and then the Saracens; their last remnants finally settled around the Pyrenees. The Ostrogoths also invaded Italy, where they were not decisively defeated until the sixth century. Most of them were then absorbed into the population; but some returned to the Crimea, where even in the sixteenth century their descendants were still speaking the ancestral tongue. In the north, meanwhile, the Angles, Frisians, Jutes, and Saxons crossed the North Sea to Britain, to be followed in the eighth to eleventh centuries by the raids and the invasions of the Vikings.

To the east, the next most powerful newcomers were the Slavs, who from the second century AD onwards had begun their long trek to the west and south, pushing into Poland, Czechoslovakia, and Germany, and down through Hungary into the Balkans. They also went north-westwards, displacing a number of smaller hunting and fishing tribes of the Finno-Ugrian family, who now went on into Finland, in turn driving further north the indigenous Lapps.

Throughout the centuries that followed, pressure from the east continued; but now its main effect was to stiffen resistance and provoke retaliation. Only two further Asian peoples seem to have been swiftly assimilated – the Bulgars in the sixth century, and the Magyars in the ninth and tenth. More characteristic in their outcome were the successive onslaughts of the Huns, Avars, Turks, and Mongols.

Pressure – and armed help – from the Asiatic Huns had already been responsible for invasions of the Roman Empire by the Goths. Then, in the fifth century, the Huns overcame the Ostrogoths and the Alans of the steppes, and pressed on into France and Italy before they were finally crushed in 454. Behind them came the partly Europeanized Avars, who at their most powerful overran eastern Europe from the Volga to the Elbe and the Baltic; not until the late eighth century were they in turn thrown back. The Turks, although they had led the sixth-century Bulgar invasion, made their first serious assaults on Europe 500 years later; and in the centuries that followed they not only defeated the Byzantine Empire, but were constantly at war across Europe's eastern borders, leaving in the Balkans a legacy of monuments and bitterness that survives to this day. The Mongols of the Golden Horde, finally, poured into eastern Europe and almost to the Adriatic in the thirteenth century; but they too at length retreated after the death of their leader, Genghis Khan.

Jews, originally from Palestine; Iberian Moors, more Berber than Arab; Gipsies, probably from north-west India; Gallicized Normans, who conquered England, invaded Italy, and led some of the Crusades; negroes from Africa and the Caribbean; Indians and Pakistanis; formerly Dutch Indonesians – these and a few others complete the long tally of peoples who have contributed to the population of Europe today. From the pithecanthropines onwards, nothing could be more varied. In the vast perspective of history, the Europeans are mongrels indeed.

Here and there, especially in isolated regions, their appearance still recalls their distant past. Seemingly Cro-Magnon features are found in Spain, parts of southern France, Germany, and southern Sweden; the Guanchos of the Canary Islands are said to embody them most fully. The very tall inhabitants of Albania and Jugoslavia, many of them over six feet, are by no means necessarily direct descendants of Cro-Magnon man; but they almost certainly owe their physical stature to the fact that the slightly-built farming newcomers from Asia Minor penetrated less far into these parts of the Balkans. In Scandinavia, again, the hunting and fishing past is recalled by present-day diet; the average Dane, Swede, or Norwegian still eats more than twice as much fish in a year as anyone else in western Europe except the Portuguese. On Europe's northern and western edges, where farming came late in the day, men's teeth still tend to be larger than in southern and eastern Europe, early adapted to vegetable and cereal foods. In remote parts of Albania and in Montenegro, theer are still men whose incisors meet in an edge-to-edge bite, instead of overlapping like those of most modern Europeans, whose molars do most of the work. The same feature was found in England and other parts of northwest Europe as late as the Norman Conquest; and it may account for the presence in English of the dental fricative "th" sound that Frenchmen, Dutchmen, and others find so hard to pronounce.

There are similar possible traces of some of the various peoples who brought farming to Europe. Leaving aside the fact that many Mediterranean housewives still look like barrel-shaped Maltese goddesses, some of today's Sicilians, south Italians, and southern French still resemble the small, slim, narrow-skulled, fine-featured people who brought shell-decorated pottery to these same shores. The irregular two-field system of farming, still followed in parts of the Mediterranean area, seems to date back to the later part of the same epoch. Further north, many east Europeans still have the stocky build, high-vaulted skulls, and short low-bridged Khrushchev noses that were typical of the "Danubian" invaders. The fair hair and pale eyes of many present-day Poles may have just as long an ancestry; while the tall, muscular "Battle-axe People", with their narrow skulls and long faces, certainly seem to have resembled some of today's north Germans and Scandinavians, in whose lands they finally settled.

Resemblances such as these have led many anthropologists into a quest for what at least three of them have called "the races of Europe". Strictly speaking, this is a misnomer. Man is one species: the only "race" in that sense is the human race.

Even the so-called major or primary "races" are clusters of people, populations with slightly differing genetic make-up, but sharing 90 per cent of their genes with the whole of mankind. However, genetic theory does not remove observable differences: it merely puts them in perspective; and many attempts have been made to arrange them in plausible groups. Any European who has applied for a United States visa will have met a sample of antiquated racial doctrine when asked to describe himself as "Caucasian". Perhaps to the relief of immigration officials, this term has little to do with the Caucasus. It refers only to a skull once found there, used by an eighteenth-century German doctor, Johann Friedrich Blumenbach, as a point of reference for what he thought were typically European features: "colour, white; cheeks rosy; hair brown or chestnut; head 'sub-globular'; face oval and straight, with its parts moderately well-defined; forehead smooth; nose narrow and slightly aquiline; mouth small; the teeth perpendicular to each jaw; the lips, especially the lower one, fairly full; the chin prominent and round." A commercial artist could hardly have bettered this hero of a boys' adventure-story or an advertisement for rugged knitwear.

Some of the classifications proposed since Blumenbach's day have been relatively simple, dividing Europeans into pale and dark, or round-headed and long. Others are more elaborate; one – which claimed to identify "Aryans" – proved tragically dangerous. But the "classic" system was that published in 1899 by the American sociologist William Z. Ripley, who saw Europeans as belonging to three main ethnic groups. The first, confined to north-west Europe, was the "Teutonic" – tall, long-headed, long-faced, thin-nosed, and blond. The second, from central Europe, was the "Alpine" or "Celtic" – stockier, round-headed, broad-faced, short-nosed, and chestnut-haired, with grey or hazel eyes. The "Mediterranean", finally, was said to be of medium height, slender, long-headed, long-faced, and fairly broad-nosed, with dark hair and eyes. This classification, with variants, is the basis of almost all later systems, as well as of much journalism, many travel books, a number of patriotic poems, and a great deal of political prejudice.

A moment's reflection, indeed, and the stereotypes take shape. See the tall Teuton from the Nordic lands, with his blond hair flying, his frank blue eyes, his grave, long face, and his manly handshake. See the short, dark, secretive Celt, with his slow cunning and untrustworthy brown eyes. See the slick, sloe-eyed Mediterranean with his short, ruttish body, his fluent gestures, and his greasy black hair. How long does it take to efface such glib absurdities? Was Dag Hammarskjold a Teuton? Is Alexander Dubček a Celt? How Mediterranean, in this sense, is Sophia Loren?

Nor are individuals the only exceptions. Blue eyes are not always found with blond hair, even home-grown and untinted: in Poland and White Russia there are many brown-eyed blonds. Many Englishmen are hardly "Teutons"; yet they are hardly diminutive "Celts". *"Non Angli, sed anguli"* was one Mediterranean's apocryphal reaction to his first tall, bony British visitor; and many a supposedly "Celtic" tourist – even from Wales – has towered above a central-European crowd. Stature, in fact, has been shown to depend partly on nourishment: many "Mediterranean" immigrant families in America have gained several inches in a generation.

In reality, the differences between Europeans are both simpler and more complex than traditional categories suggest.

A comparison of Europeans' height roughly confirms the existing picture, as does the colour of their hair and eyes. With the Balkan exceptions already specified, the tallest men and women tend to come from north-west Europe, and especially from Iceland, the Highlands of Scotland, and north-east England. The shortest are found in Sardinia, southern Italy, and central Spain. The rest of the Iberian peninsula, Italy, and most of France, have a slightly taller population; slightly taller still is that of the broad central belt stretching from eastern central France as far as central Russia. Similarly, the palest hair and eyes tend to be found in Iceland, the British Isles except Wales and the West Country, Scandinavia, Finland, northern central Europe, and Poland. The darkest are in a broad area covering the Black Sea and Caspian regions, the whole of the Balkans, southern Switzerland, Italy, Spain and Portugal, and all but the north-eastern part of France.

Head-shapes, on the other hand, partly contradict the stereotype. The longest heads, certainly, are found in Iceland, the British Isles, Sweden, Denmark, north Germany, and northern Holland; but they also occur in Spain and Portugal, in Corsica, Sardinia, and Sicily, in what used to be Latvia, and in a small enclave in central Russia. The roundest heads appear in a broad area, roughly wedge-shaped, stretching from near Bordeaux through much of central and southern Europe, round into Jugoslavia and Albania; but they are also found in Lapland, in the Caucasus, in much of Anatolia, in eastern Russia, and in an odd isolated band across the neck of the Breton peninsula.

The distribution of long and short faces shows a slightly different pattern. The longest are seen in the British Isles, Scandinavia, northern central Europe, Poland, Spain, Corsica, Sardinia, and Sicily, southern Italy, and parts of Greece; the broadest in Lapland, the Massif Central, the Alps, and the central Balkans.

When blood groups are considered, the picture grows still more complex. Of the A, B, and O groups, the commonest is O. This occurs most often in Europe's outlying areas – in Iceland, Ireland, the Basque Country, and the Caucasus. The A group is common in western Europe, but especially in Scandinavia, the Alps, and the southern and north-western parts of the Iberian peninsula. B, finally, is concentrated mostly in eastern Europe, and becomes more frequent further east; in the Pyrenees and parts of Scandinavia it remains exceptionally rare.

In some respects, these data support the traditional classification; but they also confirm that Europe's peoples, in the west especially, are as intermingled as their history suggests. If maps for the distribution of each physical feature are superimposed, the dividing lines for any one category continually interweave with those for all the others: the result is a jig-saw puzzle refuting all but the most detailed, complicated statements or – at the other extreme – the broadest of generalizations. Even so, four cardinal facts stand out.

First, almost all living Europeans have cousins or "cousins-in-law", if not ancestors, in common. It would take a good computer, an enormous field team, and a demented enthusiast for European unity, to even attempt to prove such distant connexions; but travel and interbreeding over the millennia and the centuries make the kinship of Europeans virtually certain. In a very general sense, too, they may share some common qualities. Like their descendants the Americans, they too were originally immigrants – partly pre-selected, therefore, as men of proud, restless, aggressive, competitive energy. Throughout their history they have shown it, pressing on through wild seas and cold, unfriendly mountains; taming a landscape not always hospitable; using their great ingenuity to make tools, weapons, and machines to offset their physical weakness; winning colonial empires; struggling in claustrophobic rivalry for transient power and riches, but now and then precariously allied against further invaders of their wealthy, crowded promontory on the west of the Asian landmass.

Secondly, as a corollary to their kinship, almost all Europeans – except for a few marooned for centuries in the mountains – have a highly complicated ancestry. Some, like the British, the Germans, the Italians, and the Hungarians, are more mixed than others; but there are scarcely any who could reasonably claim to be of "pure" descent.

Thirdly, the European melting-pot has not made for uniformity among its peoples. Instead, it has so juggled the variables and blended the genes as to produce immense diversity. As Europe's landscape is a mass of contrasts crammed into a small space, so are the Europeans themselves: with so many strains to draw upon, their individual variety is almost infinite.

Finally, Europe's so-called races and her real physical types bear very little relation to present-day nationalities. Traditional ethnic groups and observable human categories cover areas at once too broad and too narrow to coincide with any nation-state. Only very rarely, as in the case of the Albanians and Montenegrins, do they even approximate to the outlines of today's political entities. Elsewhere, each category sprawls over several nations, and each nation includes most categories. Almost all the sizeable nations of western Europe have greater differences within them than the average differences between them: nationality covers a multitude of sons.

These facts are obvious on any taxonomic map of Europe; but experience makes them vivid. One Icelander I know looks and sounds like a Scotsman; one English peer could pass for a typical Swede. Prominent "Dutch" teeth occur in East Anglia as well as in northern Germany. So too do sing-song long-drawn-out "ah" sounds: heard through the filter of waking, men's voices outside my Cambridge bedroom used to sound very like those of Dutchmen. In Germany in the 1960s, when well-groomed girls caught the eye of the foreign press, this was partly because they looked like trim Italians, dark, pert, buxom, and large-eyed. It was Germany's taxonomic miracle: the pig-tailed blonde *Hausfrau* had apparently dived back into the genetic pool. In southern Europe, finally, even ethnic dogmatists admit that "Mediterraneans" of all nationalities look alike, from Istanbul to Oporto. The "Teutonic"-looking classical Greeks of ancient public-school legend were probably no less swarthy than the rest. And yet, in southern Italy and Sicily, there are still men with blue eyes and ginger hair, sometimes thought to be the descendants of Norman crusaders, but perhaps the product merely of mutation in the genes.

The unity and diversity that mark Europe, then, also mark the Europeans. Other continents have other qualities. The endlessly busy activity of Europe is not always attractive; but like that of Japan today it gets results. Some are not always happy: Europeans have been responsible for appalling cruelty and suffering. But they have also put much of their energy into organization – constructing complex societies based on laws and institutions, trying to keep the peace between opposing factions. One form of society – and often one opposing faction – is the nation, gradually evolving from tribe, kingdom, or empire into something resembling the modern state. Nations, as has been seen, have little ethnic identity; but their cultural roots are very deep. The deepest of all is probably language – that long and vital taproot from which some have fashioned a conductor's baton, and some a sorcerer's wand.

4

Warring Tongues

I am always sorry when any language is lost, because languages are the pedigree of nations.

DR SAMUEL JOHNSON, quoted by James Boswell,
The Journal of a Tour to the Hebrides

LANGUAGE, like truth in Oscar Wilde's epigram, is rarely pure and never simple.

Observe a small child. Its first sound is an indignant, anguished yell. It repeats this, sometimes more quietly, whenever it wants food. Satisfied, it may purr like a cat. Soon, its crying becomes varied: an ear-splitting scream when it hurts itself badly, followed by a frenzied silence, trying to draw breath, then by repeated outraged, miserable bawling; a hiccuping grizzle when it feels hard done by, pitying itself and demanding comfort; a sobbing, testy wail when disappointed, holding the high notes longer when more angry. Frustration of various kinds may provoke violent gestures or stamping; but it also often produces a shrill growl or an expletive cry. The sounds of pleasure develop likewise: a fat chuckle, a shout of excitement, a coo of wonder, vague crooning, chanting, babbling, and muttering, or an uncontrollably gleeful *fou rire*.

Requests may be made by repeated "ah" sounds in an interrogative tone, sometimes with a clap of the hands when asking to be lifted; pointing can be imperious, or simply a desire to share. Imitation becomes important: "wough, wough" may greet a dog or any similar animal; tongue-clicking may mean horses; "dak" any bird, from mallards to magpies; a playful moan, some smaller crying baby. Already, in the pre-speech ages, an emotional and factual vocabulary is developing; and its sources and resources are surprisingly complex.

Man, inventing language, lacked the help enjoyed by most babies today; but the springs of speech have probably always been as mixed. Some sounds were no doubt cries of pain or pleasure; some were calls for help or attention; some were made to synchronize common efforts, like two men heaving together at a log or a large stone. In some cases, sound may have been analogous to gesture, moving the jaws, lips, and tongue to mimic eating or drinking, indicating hunger or thirst. Imitation of non-human sounds may have begun for pleasure and continued for communication; cries of warning or indication may have turned into conventions in the same way. Name-giving was a further step – godlike, as in the Bible; even more crucial was the development of articulated speech. Many theories have been advanced to "explain" its origins and growth: several are suspect; none alone is convincing. At one time, it was even believed that there had once been a single *Ursprache*, man's original universal language. Reason, and what evidence there is, make this extremely unlikely. Proof is impossible to come by, since men of a kind had probably been using speech of a kind many thousands of years before any trace of it that now survives.

The oldest of such remnants in western Europe may well be the names of certain rivers, apparently domesticated in their modern spelling, but still a mystery in any surviving or reconstructed idiom. Such are the Ayr or the Shiel in Scotland, with their apparent affinities to the German Ahr and the Dutch Aar or the French Seille; the Yelm in Devon and the Etruscan Alma; or the Ure in Yorkshire and the German Isar.

Similar, perhaps later, survivals are some of the countless languages of the Caucasus, and that strange Iberian anomaly, Basque – although this has occasional links with later arrivals, for instance using the word *sei* for "six".

With these main exceptions, nearly all the languages now used in Europe are derived from "Indo-European", a hypothetical family of dialects that seems to have entered the continent some 5,000 years ago with some of the later farming immigrants from the Middle East. Comparative philologists have worked hard to reconstruct some notion of "Indo-European" by noting, for instance, those words in its later derivatives that are similar enough to suggest a common source. The vocabulary thus arrived at seems to have included names for snow, ice, frost, and winter; for beech, birch, and willow; and for bear, wolf, beaver, otter, squirrel, marten, bee, and honey. It apparently lacked words for sea, palm-tree, bamboo, lion, tiger, elephant, or monkey. Probably, therefore, those who spoke the "Indo-European" dialects came from – or soon moved into – a wooded hinterland in the north temperate zone. This could conceivably have been southern Russia, between Rumania and the Urals. Similar evidence suggests that they kept oxen, sheep, goats, pigs, and dogs, and that they tamed wild horses. Some of them were probably nomadic, but others were more settled. They seem to have had no word for "trade": to "buy", in their terms, was primarily to "buy out" a bondsman or a slave. Their notions of a "guest", a "stranger", a "partner in barter", and an "enemy" were significantly related. Their society – again on linguistic evidence – was a tripartite, patriarchal structure of priests, warriors, and farmers. Not all of them had a word for "king". But they had an elaborate religious system, and they recognized property and law. Many of present-day Europe's fundamental notions, in other words, already existed in embryo 5,000 years ago.

With time, the "Indo-European" dialects divided. One important early divergence was between those that retained a hard initial "k" sound and those in which it was softened to "s" or "sh". In the former case, the original word for "a hundred", which may have been "km'tom", was modified into the Italic *cen*, the Latin *centum*, the Greek *hekaton*, the Scots Gaelic *ciad*, the Welsh *cant*, and – with a shift from "k" to "h" – the Gothic *hund*, father of *hundert* and *hundred*. In other cases, the same hypothetical word became *satam* in Sanskrit, *šimtas* in Lithuanian, and *sto* in Russian. This was perhaps the beginning of a linguistic dividing-line between western and eastern Europe.

But other cleavages were to follow. The "k" group split into Italic, Hellenic, Celtic, and "Germanic" or "Gothonic"; the "s" or "sh" group into Baltic, Slavonic, Albanian, and Armenian. Most of these then divided again. Of today's living languages, Italic gave birth to the Latin group – Provençal, Catalan, Spanish, Portuguese, French, Italian, Romansh, and Rumanian. Celtic produced Irish, Welsh, Gaelic, and Breton – this last through British influence. Northern "Gothonic" led to Icelandic, Faroese, Norwegian, Danish, and Swedish; western "Gothonic" was the ancestor of High German, Low German, Letzeburgesch, Dutch and Flemish, Frisian, and English. From Baltic came Latvian and Lithuanian; from east Slavonic, Russian, White Russian, and Ukrainian; from west Slavonic, Polish, Pomeranian, Czech, Slovak, and Wendish; and from south Slavonic, Bulgarian, Macedonian, Serbo-Croat, and Slovene.

Outside the "Indo-European" family, finally – although perhaps related to its remoter antecedents – is the Finno-Ugrian group of languages, today represented chiefly by Estonian, Finnish, Lappish, Magyar, Ostyak, Permian, Vogul, and Volga Finnic.

Such is the classical picture of Europe's linguistic family tree, based mainly on analysis of vocabulary. This, of course, is not the only criterion. Sounds and speech-tunes also give clues to linguistic genealogy. Some, like the differences between Spanish, French, and Italian, may reflect the previous speech habits of those who adopted "Indo-European" derivatives; some, like the "th" sounds in English and Icelandic, may be survivals from quite early offshoots such as Celtic; some, like the "Geordie" intonations of Newcastle or the long vowels of East Anglia, may result from the later influence of Norse or Dutch. Some may be fairly recent transplants, like the dry velar "r" of Danish, which originated in seventeenth-century Paris, was adopted by the Prussian court of Frederick II, and then spread to the German-speaking Danish nobility. A still more recent instance is American influence on English, affecting not only vocabulary but also pronunciation, as in the shortening of the "ah" sound, and the opening of the short English "o" as in "got" into something more like the American vowel, midway between "gaht" and "gut". Nor, indeed, are these the only indications of lingustic kinship. Recent comparisons of grammatical structure may yet reveal links and contrasts hitherto unsuspected.

Already it is clear, then, that most of the languages spoken in Europe today are cousins – which puts the quest for linguistic "purity" firmly in perspective. And yet, even so, the quest continues. Nor, within limits, is it without point.

In the early 1960s, Professor René Etiemble of the Sorbonne published a best-selling polemic entitled *Parlez-vous franglais? "Vous serez relax!"* proclaimed its cover, quoting an advertisement; and the book went on to point out how modern French was being "invaded" by terms like *"le drugstore"*, *"le quick-lunch"*, *"le bodygraph"*, and *"le snack"*. It showed, too, that in the process of borrowing from English, sense and consistency were often lost. Why should "walking" become *"le footing"* and "footing", or status, *"le standing"*? Why should a tennis-player be *"un tennisman"*? Should *"knickerbockers"* be singular or plural? How should one wear *"un short"* or *"un pull"*? Why have thirteen different ways of spelling *"le sheriff"*? How should a Frenchman pronounce *"le yachting"* – like "yak" or like "yashmak"? Why should *"un bottle-party"* be masculine, but *"une cheese-party"* feminine? Should the French for "beefsteak" be spelt with a *c* or a *q*, or with neither? How would one cook "a beefsteak of veal"?

Alongside these importations, French words themselves were losing precision and nuance. Like "disinterested" in English, now taken by many to mean "uninterested" rather than "impartial", words like *"offense"*, *"réaliser"*, or *"actuellement"*, which used to be traps for the hasty translator, were taking on the meanings of their once "false friends". Even the word *"arriviste"*, semi-naturalized in English, was giving way to *"carriériste"*, modelled on "careerist" – probably from the United States.

Examples like these – and others from the world of publicity, such as *"chocorêve"*, *"télébrité"*, and *"univerchelle"* – made it easy to sympathize with Etiemble. But the process he deplored has a very long history. In *Le Père Goriot*, first published in 1835, Balzac had already ridiculed the vogue for the suffix *"-rama"*, which Etiemble still found rife in *"amusorama"*, *"cityrama"*, *"stripperama"*, and *"sexyrama"*. And while expressions like *"le weekend"* or *"le living"* (for "living-room") may be recent, such anglicisms as *"le smoking"* and *"le shake-hand"* – or *"le shampooing"*, borrowed via English from the Hindi *"champna"* – could hardly now be considered wholly alien.

Languages, like people, seldom borrow or adopt without reason. As Ezra Pound once remarked, "the sum of human wisdom is not contained in any one language, and no single language is CAPABLE of expressing all forms and degrees of human comprehension." If only for this reason, the quest for total "purity" seems doomed. In Europe, only two countries have come really close to achieving it – Lithuania and Iceland, the latter by deliberately excluding a number of Danish expressions. And while English is perhaps the biggest borrower of foreign words, French too has drawn extensively, not only on its Latin roots but also on Greek, Arabic, Hindi, Slav, and other varied sources. One of the words that Etiemble used most frequently, *"le sabir"* – in the phrase *"le sabir atlantique"* as a synonym for *"franglais"* – is itself of Spanish extraction, and used to describe a mixed patois spoken in North Africa and the Levant.

Warring Tongues

Seafarers have always shared odds and ends of terminology – as witness, in English, Dutch nautical terms like "boom" and "skipper"; and traders, in particular, have often found themselves inventing mixed or improvised languages, such as pidgin (for "business") English. But the best-publicized artificial languages are the work of late-nineteenth-century idealists: Volapük, devised by a German pastor, Johann Martin Schleyer, in 1879; and Esperanto, proposed eight years later by Dr Lazarus Ludovic Zamenhof, an oculist from Warsaw. Both built their vocabularies by borrowing from Romance and Germanic languages. Volapük is inflectional, and includes invented vocabulary and syntax; even the words it took over from living languages it transformed, as in its own title, a corruption and combination of "world" and "speech". Although adopted by some educational experts, it finally failed to live up to its name – partly owing to copyright disputes. Esperanto, whose author renounced all right of control or ownership, has been more successful. Less rigid and bizarre than Volapük, it incorporates many existing words, spelt phonetically in a twenty-eight letter alphabet, with fixed endings for different parts of speech – "o" for nouns, "a" for adjectives, and "e" for adverbs. Hearing or reading it, a non-Esperantist feels rather like someone with a smattering of Italian paying his first visit to Spain or Rumania. The Lord's Prayer in Esperanto reads as follows:

Patro nia, kiu estas en la ĉielo, Sankta estu Via nomo, Venu reĝeco Via, Estu volo Via, kiel en la ĉielo, tiel ankaŭ sur la tero. Panon nian ĉiutagan donu al ni hodiaŭ; Kaj pardonu al ni ŝuldojn niajn, Kiel ni ankaŭ pardonas al niaj ŝuldantoj; Kaj ne konduku nin en tenton, Sed liberigu nin de malbono. Ĉar Via estas la regado, la forto, kaj la gloro, eterne. Amen.

Clearly, even novices here can vaguely understand each other; but although Esperanto has a weird sonorous dignity lacking in, say, the New English Bible, it and its successors – including Ido, or revised Esperanto, and Interglossa – still seem no more than ingenious efforts in a valiant but lost cause.

Not that any language is wholly "natural": made-up expressions like "television", "spacecraft", "bulldozer", "air-conditioning", or "Eurocrat" have been adopted very widely. Flying already has its *lingua franca*, largely Anglo-American, in the air and on the ground. So do science, technology, and business management; so does sport. Less conspicuously, the multinational institutions of the Common Market are gradually developing a modern administrative *sabir* compounded from French, German, Italian, and even English, although Britain's full weight in this respect has yet to be felt. Stylistically, it has its drawbacks: but its concision is often too tempting to resist. *"Conjoncture"* is a neat way of saying "the present state of the economic cycle". *"Sprachregelung"* crisply expresses "the general line to take in a public statement". *"Ridimensionamento"* puts into one word "a change of scale that alters proportional differences"; and no other language has yet produced short synonyms for "timing" or "package deal". If Europeans in the future come to share more of a common language, it will probably be in such ways as this. Necessity and convenience are more powerful than grammarians or visionaries. Every new idiom is a kind of Desperanto.

All these are extreme examples; but no language is completely free of foreign loan-words, most of them now perfectly at home. Nor can any of Europe's major living languages be totally identified with a single nation. Dynastic marriages, inheritance, purchase, diplomatic wrangling, and even donation – all have helped to determine political frontiers, even after the dispersal of Europe's peoples and the emergence from their ancestral languages of something like the present linguistic map. Royal marriages have brought together job lots of territory, people, and language: Poland and Hungary; Poland and Lithuania; Poland and East Prussia; Hungary and Bohemia; Hungary and Croatia; Hungary and Austria; Spain and the Low Countries; Sweden and Norway; Norway and Denmark; much of France and England; England and Hanover. In cases where rulers were elected, religion or local rivalry was sometimes more important in the choice of a monarch than language or nationality: Russia was long governed by princes of Scandinavian origin; Poland had French, Rumanian, Swedish, and German kings. Many lands were simply conquered; Corsica was actually purchased; diplomatic pressure secured the South Tyrol for Italy; and a princely gesture by Napoleon III gave back to the Italian royal family the Tenda hunting-grounds in the maritime Alps.

At the Paris peace conference of 1919, attempts were made to "Keep Europe Tidy". Especially in the east, the old dynastic frontiers were replaced by others, thought to be more in keeping with nationality, viability, and security. Germany ceded territory to France, Belgium, Denmark, Lithuania, Czechoslovakia, and Poland. The Austro-Hungarian empire was divided, parts of it going to Austria, Hungary, Czechoslovakia, Poland, Rumania, Jugoslavia, and Italy. During World War II, eastern Europe saw huge forced migrations and, later, floods of refugees. After the war, even in the west, there were further shifts of frontier. Italy's northern borders were once again adjusted; the Saar passed back and forth between France and Germany. Germany was divided, and its eastern frontiers moved west, giving territory to Poland, which in turn gave its eastern lands to Russia. East Prussia, Estonia, Latvia, and Lithuania also now became part of the Soviet Union, as did portions of Czechoslovakia, Rumania, and Finland.

Centuries of such practical map-making have led to many anomalies. In Western Europe alone, not counting such special cases as Belgium and Switzerland, there are some thirty small communities, most of them with their own language or patois, that are still not fully assimilated into their respective nation-states. If all the members of these linguistic minorities were to join forces, they would form a polyglot nation of well over eight million people – more than Sweden or Switzerland, and almost as many as Belgium. Individually, their numbers range from 12,000 or so Slovenes in Austria to several million Catalans in Spain; they include not only such active groups as the

Welsh or Gaelic-speaking Scots in Britain and the Alsatians, Basques, and Bretons in France, but also less well known minorities like the Greeks of southern Italy, the German-speaking communities in northern Schleswig, Denmark, and the half-million Frisians in the Netherlands.

Despite their numbers, dispersal and disunity make these millions of Europeans weak *vis-à-vis* the nation-states that include them. To the cool outside observer, and to some of the national majorities, their situation may seem like a piece of irritating folklore; but for many of the minorities it remains a real plight. Some, as in Denmark and Germany, are well treated, with fair facilities for educating their children and playing their part in national life. Others fare less well, as in the South Tyrol or in France, where until recently any inhabitants of Brittany who baptized their children with Breton names were denied family allowances – because, the authorities told them, children without French Christian names did not legally exist. Even in a country like Belgium, where Flemish and French are now theoretically equal, it used to be said that in a typical Brussels business firm the doorman would speak only Flemish, the secretaries would be bilingual, and the managing director would speak only French. In recent years, backed by a rising birth-rate and rapid economic growth, the Flemings have pressed harder for equality, sometimes overstating their case. The French-speaking Walloons of southern Belgium, with its older and often declining industries, are now on the defensive. Although outside Belgium their mother tongue is more useful than Flemish, they resent French predominance and some Frenchmen's sneers at their accent. At home, they are still reluctant to learn Flemish, which sounds to many of them uncouth; yet they fear that without it they will not only be outnumbered – as they are already – but also lose jobs to bilingual Flemings. In Brussels, a largely French-speaking enclave in the midst of Flemish Brabant, the tensions are as great as anywhere: some extremists have even compared Brussels to Berlin.

In situations like these, language problems enter every

crevice of daily life – at home, at school, at work, in shops, in cafés, in the bank or the post office, in dealings with public officials from policemen to hospital staff. The pains and indignities of linguistic alienation are real and deep. They go deepest of all when, as sometimes happens, they affect the family: what children learn at school, and in what language, has often proved a flashpoint where fear and desperation turn to violence. The whole subject, in fact, is too explosive and intimate to be left to chance or haggling. There is still some point in the mediaeval doctrine that a man's speech expresses his soul.

"When I was little," confessed Jean Cocteau, "I believed that foreigners could not really talk at all, but were only pretending." Even some adults, especially in France, Britain, and the United States, still seem to feel, if not to claim, that theirs is the best, perhaps the only authentic language; that nuances which it finds hard or impossible to express are without any true significance; that the world's complexity is faithfully mirrored by the vocabulary and grammar that they know. Not everyone is so naïve; but most people, puzzled by a complex statement in a foreign tongue, are likely to ask without any sense of irony, "What does that *really* mean?"

As the German satirist Karl Kraus remarked, "speech is the mother of thought, not its handmaiden." One psychologist has coined the term "metalinguistics" to denote the implications of language, reaching into epistemology, metaphysics, religion, ethics, sociology, politics, and art. Others have suggested that even languages of the same extended family, like most of those in Europe, provide clues to the various peoples who speak them – not only by expressing their supposed "ethnic character", but also by shaping the very nature of their thoughts and feelings. "Every language," wrote Georges Mounin, "has its latent ideology. Each one chooses different aspects of reality, and we see in the universe only what our language points out." The French philologist Joseph Vendryes even believed that the habit of always putting the verb in a certain place makes for a certain way of thinking, and may have some influence on how a line of argument develops. French, German, and English thought is in some degree subordinate to language. A light, flexible language, whose grammar is minimal, allows thought to appear in all its clarity, and enables it to move freely; thought is hindered, on the other hand, by the constraints of one that is ponderous and rigid.

By "light" and "flexible", Vendryes may have meant "familiar", if not "French" – although a British reader might plump for "English". Did he, by "ponderous" and "rigid", mean German? He failed to explain. But, prejudice apart, he also failed to pursue the argument. "To seek the spirit of a people through the character of its language," he concluded, "is a hopeless task in the present state of our facilities for research."

Hopeless the quest may be: but many bold spirits have attempted it. One of the first was the German poet Johann Gottfried von Herder, in his *Treatise on the Origin of Language*, published in 1772. Interest in the subject might almost seem a trait of national character, since similar efforts were made by Karl Wilhelm von Humboldt, whose study of the Basque language appeared in 1821, as well as by several later German philologists and philosophers. The most celebrated of these, if not always the most modest, was Count Hermann Alexander Keyserling. In 1928, in his *Das Spektrum Europas*, he paraded some plausible impressions – of the British (spiritual, lazy, and hostile to thought), the French (intellectual), the Spaniards (fanatical), the Germans (scholarly), the Italians (theatrical), the Swiss (parochial), the Dutch (brutish but cultured), the Belgians (showy), the Swedes (good-natured), the Russians (un-European), the Balkans (restless), the Greeks (austere), and the Turks (idle, autocratic, and formidable). Keyserling complained that "it was precisely the English critics who reproached me with 'lacking a sense of humour'." "I could never understand why," he declared – although in earlier years he had founded what he called "The School of

Wisdom". Then, light dawned. "I perceived that this was their way of dismissing something that made them feel uncomfortable." Perhaps it was. But alongside many additions to the museum of national clichés, to be inspected in the next chapter, Keyserling made some fair intuitive points. The English language, he felt, was resolute, reserved, and personal; French was calm, lucid, measured. The sonorous metallic ring of Castilian Spanish suggested proud and passionate energy. German combined solid strength with fluid feeling.

Slightly more systematic, and certainly more self-critical, are the further intuitive insights of another amateur philologist, Don Salvador de Madariaga. The son of a Spanish army officer, and originally trained as a civil engineer, Madariaga adorned many professions before qualifying as an international sage. His recreation, he admitted, was "a change of work". Five years a journalist in London, and for a time a civil servant with the League of Nations, he was appointed Professor of Spanish Studies at Oxford in 1928, then Spanish Ambassador to the United States in 1931 and to France in 1932. After the Franco revolution, he devoted his time to teaching and writing outside Spain. His books range from scholarly studies of disarmament and international relations to a lively novel, *The Heart of Jade*, which pleased sex-starved barrack-rooms in 1944. In 1952, when he first published his *Portrait of Europe*, he quoted in the foreword the peroration of a speech he had made at the Hague congress on European unity four years earlier:

Above all, we must love Europe; our Europe, sonorous with the roaring laughter of Rabelais, luminous with the smile of Erasmus, sparkling with the wit of Voltaire; in whose mental skies shine the fiery eyes of Dante, the clear eyes of Shakespeare, the serene eyes of Goethe, the tormented eyes of Dostoievski; this Europe to whom La Gioconda for ever smiles, where Moses and David spring to perennial life from Michelangelo's marble, and Bach's genius rises spontaneous to be caught in his intellectual geometry; where Hamlet seeks in thought the mystery of his inaction, and Faust seeks in action comfort for the void in his thought; where Don

Juan seeks in women the woman never found, and Don Quixote, spear in hand, gallops to force reality to rise above itself; this Europe where Newton and Leibniz measure the infinitesimal, and the Cathedrals, as Musset once wrote, pray on their knees in their robes of stone; where rivers, silver threads, link together strings of cities, jewels wrought in the crystal of space by the chisel of time ... this Europe must be born. And she will, when Spaniards will say "our Chartres", Englishmen "our Cracow", Italians "our Copenhagen"; when Germans say "our Bruges", and step back horror-stricken at the idea of laying murderous hands on it. Then will Europe live, for then it will be that the Spirit that leads History will have uttered the creative words: FIAT EUROPA!

Here, certainly, Madariaga confirmed the stereotype of the Spaniard. No one could be more passionate or lyrical in the cause of a united Europe; and few could be as cavalier with reality. The chisel of time still has work to do on such jewels as Slough. But Madariaga's enthusiasm by no means blinded him to the contrasts between Europeans; and he pointed out profound linguistic differences with much shrewdness and wit.

Many of his views on language are debatable. Not everyone would agree that "the prevalence of the letter 'e' in the French language", flattening into *"père"* and *"mère"* the rounder vowels of *"pater"* and *"mater"*, is in itself a mark of French "measure" and "equilibrium"; that Spanish passion is expressed by "the prevalence of the full vowels, 'o' and 'a' '"; that the recurrence of "i" in Italian is an indication of intent acuteness and intellect; or that the frequency in German of "u" and of "Ur-" and "Um-" shows "the fluid nature of German thought". But he seems on firmer ground in recalling that when Spanish seeks to deride or belittle something, it flattens it with an "e", as in *"vejete"*, a "silly old man". Spanish words in French, on the other hand, take on an air of bombast, as in *"hâbler"*, "to brag", derived from *"hablar"*, "to speak". In Spanish ears, finally, Italian indeed seems to sound "theatrical": *"elenco"*, merely a "list" in Italy, means the "cast of a play" in Spain.

Equally evocative are some of Madariaga's remarks on the

contrasts between German, French, and English. The Germans, he declares, were originally

a people whose way of living had been for long that of wandering tribes, and who therefore were apt to look on life as something ever in flux, never to be caught and shaped inside hard and fast moulds; a people in whose collective soul ideas and feelings constantly flow out of each other in ever rolling motion, like clouds in the sky which the wind drives on, leaving them no respite to stay their course and acquire a definite profile.

The French nation, by contrast, is "always ready to shape its life into concrete and definite forms." The difference is embodied in their respective languages:

The chief feature of the German language in this respect might well be the prevalence of the word *"werden"*; that of the French language, the partitive article.... A thing in German *is* not done; it *becomes* done. This feature imparts to the language a kind of continuous motion, a sense of flow....

The French partitive article, on the other hand, as in the phrase *"de l'eau"*, makes it clear that the water in question is only a part of all the water in the universe, the abstract concept to which all instances refer back. "Thus it is that life, which for the Germans is like a river, is for the French like a string of clear cut crystals."

The contrast between English and German, in Madariaga's eyes, is something different again:

In order to say "I have dropped my glove", the German says *"Mein Handschuh ist hinuntergefallen"*.... The Englishman has reduced the number of sounds he needs to a minimum.... The sound is perfect. The image is perfect also....

Now turn to the German.... Notice the organ-like weight and sonority of the sentence, its length and that of its words.... The possessive "My" is now loaded with a heavy "n" : *"Mein"*. Instead of the light and elegant "glove", the German says *"Handschuh"*, i.e., "handshoe", a concept rather than a live word, and a heavy and ungraceful concept at that, without subtlety or humour. And finally, *"ist hinuntergefallen"*, which is over-explanatory, a whole treatise on the art of falling, of actual, effective falling, here at my feet, lest you have not understood it—a word for slow minds who need a lot of explaining.

As if this were not enough, Madariaga continues:

> English is to German as a dry sponge to a soaked one. This mushy character of the German language finds expression in the superabundance of the sound "Sch".... The swelling which so much water produces adds also to the volume of the numerous syllables in "um", "am", all heavy with mush; and, at the slightest pressure, all this water fizzles out in the words ending in "itz", like *"Spitz"*, or *"Witz"*.
>
> The German is moreover usually hot by temperament. Then, all this water tends to produce steam. Hence the frequency of the sound "f" in German, particularly at the end of the syllable. All "v"s are made to blow out steam and become "f"s. And as for "p"s they all end in "f"s, as in *"Pferde"*, *"Pfeife"*.... Thus "camp" become *"Kampf"*. And the very word for steam could not be more characteristic: *"Dampf"*.
>
> All this would appear to show that the typically German state of mind might be that hot sentimentality which finds expression in words such as *"Schwüle"* and *"Schwärmerai"*. It is hot. One breathes with difficulty. There is a lot of foam, *"Schaum"*, within. It seeks an outlet, and the language becomes a *"Dampfmaschine"* all "Schw"s and "fff"s.

Even the future, finally, becomes vague and cloudy:

> The Latin languages emphatically say "I have to do something", for that is the meaning of the future which they have shaped for themselves on original lines independently of the Latin language from which they all come: *"haré"*, *"ferai"*, *"farò"*. The English form of the future is equally definite. "I shall do it" or "I will do it". The German says: *"Ich werde es tun"*, that is: "I am becoming doing", I am flowing from this present state of not doing into a state of doing.

How much of all this is nonsense? Some, but not necessarily all. Madariaga's examples could be multiplied in several directions. French, for instance, is the analytical language *par excellence*, forcing the conscientious translator to break a concise but clotted English expression like "the detergent that washes without boiling" into its constituent elements, and write very explicitly *"la lessive qui lave sans qu'on ait besoin de faire bouillir le linge"*. "Ready-to-wear", likewise, should strictly become "ready-to-be-worn" when translated into French.

If French is clear and sometimes pedantic, Italian may sound to an English ear both "abstract" and "literary". Melodic as its vowel-sounds are, its structure and vocabulary make it seem as formal as French, even when used by so delicate and graceful a writer as Cesare Pavese or Giorgio Bassani. Closer study reveals its muscles; but, even so, it shows a concern for the aesthetic that English often lacks. Whatever the precise overtone of *"une bella criticia"*, the expression has no exact English counterpart; and from an etymological viewpoint the phrase *"fare bella figura"* may seem typically to stress the aesthetic rather than the moral aspects of "showing up well".

German, too, may seem to confirm Madariaga's impression. It sounds like a language full of force and uneasy emotion, with its *Sehnsucht* and *Schwermut* and its use of the same word – *"Schuld"* – for "debt" and for "guilt". One French observer, André Siegfried, went so far as to list what he thought were traits of German character, with the tell-tale words against each. *"Ur-"*, *"echt"*, and *"rein"*, he thought, showed a concern with the sources of things; *"Sturm und Drang"* and *"Kraft"* denoted force; flux and "becoming" were expressed by *"werden"* and *"Entwicklung"*; vagueness by words like *"Schwindel"*, *"tief"*, *"Chaos"*, and *"problematisch"*; sadism by *"Schadenfreude"* and *"Götterdämmerung"*; sentimentality by *"Heim"*, *"Heimweh"*, *"heimlich"*, *"Gemut"*, and *"Gemütlich"*; earnestness by *"tüchtig"*, *"fleissig"*, *"Ernst"*, and *"gründlich"*; objectivity by *"Wirtschaft"*, *"sachlich"*, and *"Sachlichkeit"*; a concern for the collective by *"Volk"* and *"Gemeinschaft"*; and mysticism by *"Geist"*, *"Seele"*, and *"Stimmung"*.

English, in total contrast, seems curt and bony, full of

matter-of-fact down-to-earth compounds formed from short and simple words. Its highest-prized qualities appear to be moral: its proverbial expressions warn against judging by appearances or being too clever by half. As a child, reading French fairy-tales, I was surprised at how often their heroes were described as "intelligent" – a word which in English I had heard most often applied to dogs.

Similar impressions can be gleaned from other languages. Does the untranslatable *"deftig"* – a blend of "upright", "respectable", "superior", and "slightly stiff" – not say something about the proud propriety of many Dutchmen, or the self-righteousness of South African Boers? Do the moaning, uncertain speech-tunes of Sweden suggest a tortured Nordic soul? Does the flat "Brummagem" near-German of Letzeburgesch suit an ingrowing people in a thundery, headachey climate, too often invaded, keeping themselves to themselves?

Perhaps, but with many provisos. Most such generalizations are as hazardous as Madariaga's own.

The cut-and-dried order that he claimed to detect in French may indeed be that of a peasant, counting the crop, cleaning and storing every implement, taming nature with the straight furrows of logic. But *"paysan"* means "countryman" as well as "peasant", and it includes the elusive poacher as well as the frugal tiller of the soil. Nor, *pace* Madariaga, is French the only language to use the partitive article: but do Italians share the same philosophic bent? French, moreover, can be as spuriously precise as English can be falsely downright. A favourite word in administration and politics is *"certain"*, as in *"un certain nombre de décisions"* or *"dans certains cas"*. Here, quite obviously, the word means the opposite of what it seems to say: it masks the speaker's probable ignorance and prolongs that of his audience. Neatness and vagueness, in other words, can easily coexist.

Italian, again, with extra syllables inherited from Latin but long lost by French – as in *"padre"* for *"père"* or *"movimento"* for *"mouvement"* – can certainly seem florid and theatrical; but its "abstract" sound to Englishmen or Americans is simply due to its lack of non-Latin derivatives. English uses Latinisms chiefly to be abstract; Italian, like other Romance languages, has to use them to be concrete as well.

Nor is German necessarily vague and shifting, as a session with a company lawyer will quickly show. Its apparent fluidity may seem to echo the music of Wagner or the early silent films of Fritz Lang; but does its use of *"werden"* as an auxiliary verb really bear all the weight that Madariaga places on it? Few Germans even say the word slowly when speaking of the future: *"Ich werde es tun"* snaps out crisply, often followed by an interjection *" – sofort!"* And André Siegfried's list of "typical" German words, evocative as it is, could be paralleled in many other languages. To build a psychological theory on these grammatical bases, or on fanciful onomatopoeia, seems rather excessive. One might almost as well argue that "the French" are "impersonal" because they say *"On y va!"* for "Let's go!" and *"Ça klaxonne"* for "Everybody's hooting". Are the British "unmusical" because they repeat their auxiliary verbs, or because so many other words have similar endings? In 1815, one cross French visitor thought so. Even then, the argument was far-fetched.

Linguistic comparisons can be illuminating; but whatever dim truths they grope for, the logic involved is far too often circular. Our perception of any foreign idiom is almost always coloured by the character of our own: our preconceptions about other peoples partly determine our reaction to their language – which is then fed back to reinforce the prejudices with which we began. Over the years, the feedback is continuous. Philip Guedalla once remarked that "History repeats itself; historians repeat each other." The same is true of travellers and international sages. In the gallery of national stereotypes, travellers' and old wives' tales look suspiciously alike.

5

Rogues' Gallery

I have ever hated all nations, professions and communities, and all my love is towards individuals.

JONATHAN SWIFT, Letter to Alexander Pope,
September 29, 1725

EUROPE is a mirror-maze for tourists. Crossing the thres-
hold of national frontiers, travellers find themselves and
each other: visions loom, and shift, and vanish; shapes and
faces go awry; and a whole series of imaginary worlds comes
into being – the multiple projections of everyone's fears and
longings, superimposed to form a light-show of infinite complexity, changing with the centuries but in some way constant, and still affecting the actual behaviour of nations.

A map of the mythical Europes inside our skulls would be
even more confusing than one that tried to blend geology,
meterology, ethnology, economics, sociology, politics, language, and psychology. It would have to include the great,
legendary continental divides: between the hot, garrulous
south and the cold northern silence; between the west's frank
multiplicity and the mysterious, monolithic east. It would
trace the isopleths of Protestant permissiveness and probity,

70

and Catholic discipline and guile; of Latin authority and
Nordic democracy; of Teutonic strength and Anglo-Saxon in-
dolence. It would stress the confluence of distant friends and
the occlusion between rival neighbours. It would reveal the
outcrops of cleanliness, militarism, pride, frivolity, and bad
cooking. Almost everywhere, it would show magnetic varia-
tions, gravity anomalies, and any number of mirages.

If everyone were believed, in fact, no one could be trusted.
The endless mutual slanders that Europeans have exchanged
throughout the centuries recall the sheet of paper in the
logical conundrum, on each side of which is written: "The
statement on the other side is untrue." The perfidy of foreign
men, it seems, can only be matched by the frailty of foreign
women. Even our own dull virtue is suspect: to foreigners
we too are foreign, and even here is elsewhere somewhere
else. So we emerge from the mirror-maze, blinking in the
sunlight. But the images haunt our dreams.

Strange notions of distant peoples date from the dawn of
Europe's history. Herodotus, although a sceptic, reported tales
of one-eyed men, of a goat-footed race, and of a nation that
was bald from birth. Othello's prodigies were nothing new.
Several European languages preserve the trace of similar monsters: the Czech word for "monster" itself, *"obr"*, is a reminder of the Avars, while that for "giant" in German is
"Hüne" – a relic of the short but ruthless Huns. Milder examples from later centuries include expressions like "Dutch
courage", "German measles", *"die englische Krankheit"*
(rickets), or *"filer à l'anglaise"* ("to take French leave").

There are traces of such national or regional feeling in the
middle ages. In Alsace and Lorraine in the eleventh and
twelfth centuries, for example, Burgundians seem to have
been despised. But national stereotypes, as might be expected,
developed most fully with the rise of the nation-state. From
the fifteenth century onwards, travellers' tales and general
surveys began to multiply. Together, they provide composite
pictures of how Europe's leading nations appeared to each
other and to themselves. If the portraits make up a European

rogues' gallery, the fault is not always in the sitters. Ugliness, like beauty, is often in the eyes of the beholder. To establish this, and to offset with facts and fresh judgements some persistent legends, Germany, Italy, France, and Britain can be considered in turn.

Teutonic Night

Germany—a force of that Nature to which she clings; a bundle of strong and troubled instincts: born artists without taste, technicians who are still feudal, fathers of families who are warriors; restaurants like temples, Gothic palaces as conveniences; oppressors who want to be loved, separatists who are strictly obedient, knights bearing garlands who vomit beer; a path that Siegfried finds epic at dawn, romantic at noon, and warlike at dusk; a sublime green ocean where the net hoists a tangle of monsters and treasures; a cathedral whose many-coloured nave and arches ring with delicate sounds, making a symphony for the senses, for the mind, the soul, the feelings, the light and the religion of the world, but whose transept, strident with barbarian clamour, assaults the eyes, the spirit, and the heart.

So wrote Charles de Gaulle in *Vers l'armée de métier*, published in 1934. Then, as so often, he expressed with ambiguity and eloquence the views of the man in the street, or the woman in the concierge's *loge*. Eleven years earlier, Carl Jacob Burckhardt had had equally mixed feelings about the nature of the Germans, "at once sentimental yet scientifically and technologically so gifted and so hard-working, this nature which so easily turns to scientific barbarism." There were echoes here of World War I, when Charles Maurras had declared that barbaric savagery was "inborn in the instincts of German flesh and blood". But the accusation was no novelty. As early as the fourteenth century, Jean Froissart had alleged that German soldiers showed "no mercy or pity for any man".

An observer in the 1960s, Hermann Eich, explained this in terms of over-reaction. "The need to compensate for an enforced servility by uncouth behaviour towards others," he wrote, "is one of the most crucial German character traits." In reality, it seems universal; but Germany has long been accused of subservience. "Long legs and obedience," snorted Nietzsche; and in 1903 Romain Rolland confessed his "admiration and slight fear of the magnificent machine that Germany seems to be". Another French writer, in 1945, understandably claimed that "the German has an invincible nostalgia for 'a strong hand', an incredible submissiveness before the competence of a leader and a technician." André Siegfried, also writing after World War II, added that "in Germany there seems to be no greater pleasure than a parade."

Equally celebrated is German punctilio over rank. "Everyone," wrote Madame de Staël, "has his rank, his place, as it were his post, and no one needs ingenious turns of phrase, interjections, or hints to express his superiority of birth or title." This made conversation formal: "the most meagre title – often the longest to pronounce – is said and repeated twenty times in the course of a single meal." More than 150 years later, in 1967, a manual for British businessmen warned them that in Germany "one must remember the full title of anyone who is introduced and always refer to him by his full title. . . . On meeting, one should produce one's visiting card and shake hands long and vigorously."

The German appetite for hard work, already mentioned by Burckhardt, is as familiar as German formality. "The Germans," wrote a sixteenth-century Spanish military expert, Collado, "are phlegmatic people and do things more accurately and more patiently than the Spaniards or the Italians." "In almost everything," wrote Jules Michelet in 1842,

they are workmen. Even in the military art, they very soon had excellent soldiers, true workmen of war: slowness, routine, preoccupation with war's mechanical and automatic aspects. When the unexpected appears—a Gustavus Adolphus, a Frederick, a Napoleon—routine fails, and nothing else is left.

Nearly a century later, Havelock Ellis gave the same verdict. "In association with the comparative characterlessness of German genius," he announced, "we find also, and no doubt inevitably, a lack of originality and initiative." Goethe himself had admitted that "it is in the nature of Germans that they act heavily and that everything they touch turns to lead"; and Thomas Mann, in *Doktor Faustus* complained of "a certain squareness, rhythmic clumsiness, immobility, *grossièreté*". Madame de Staël spoke of their "slowness and inertia"; but she also acknowledged their "power to work". "They set about work as others would set about sin," remarked a World War I French prisoner. Hard work, added George Mikes, was "one of their greatest crimes". And yet in 1860, when the American traveller Bayard Taylor—now chiefly remembered for a jog-trot translation of Goethe's *Faust*—was asked what foreign qualities he could commend to his countrymen, his answer was surprising:

In one respect we might profitably imitate the Germans. Our sorest need, as a people, is recreation—relaxation of the everlasting tension of our laborious lives. Among our Teutonic cousins, a certain amount of recreation, public as well as domestic, is part of the plan of every man's life. The poorest labourer has his share—*must* have it—and the treadmill round of his years is brightened and sweetened by it. Our seasons of recreation, being so rare, too frequently take the character of excess. They are characterized by the same hurry and fury with which we prosecute our business. If we shall ever intercalate regular periods of genial relaxation into our working calendar, we shall be a healthier and happier people than we are now.

How, in the travellers' tales, does "the German" spend his periods of "genial relaxation"? In windy philosophizing, listening to music, consuming beer and sausages, and avoiding voracious women.

"There are mysteries in the German mind," wrote Philip Gibbs in 1934, "we cannot fathom or understand." Bayard Taylor himself conceded that

There is ... one element of courtesy in which the Germans are deficient. Being a people of abstract ideas, and much given to that species of theorizing which breeds intellectual egotism, they lack a proper consideration for the ideas and opinions of others. Hence, a mixed conversation very often assumes the character of an argumentative combat. I have frequently heard facts denied, because they conflicted with some pet theory. As an American and a republican, I was constantly liable to be assailed by those who advocated the monarchical system—not in the way of courteous inquiry, but direct attack. In Art, Literature, and Science, it is the same thing. The Germans have adopted the idea that the great characteristic of the American people is *Materialism*—because this forms a convenient antithesis to the German trait of Idealism—and all the facts one may adduce to prove its falsity go for nothing. So with their ideas concerning European politics. They are based upon abstract doctrines—theories of race, of "national elements"—which every year sees scattered to the winds, but, nevertheless, they put the fragments together again, and look upon the structure with the same unshaken complacency as before. This intellectual egotism is at first offensive to a stranger, and one never becomes entirely reconciled to it. The same characteristic may be observed among the various classes of ultra-reformers in the United States.

Madame de Staël had noted similar dogmatism. "Men of distinction in Germany," she wrote, "are very severe." For fear of being snubbed, "ordinary people are mostly silent, and a sort of friendly goodwill is their only contribution to sociability." "A German," therefore, "always has in his head a little more than he knows how to express."

The sense of confusion is general. A modern American professor of German history, Hans Kohn, believes that

The Germans easily succumb to the strange fascination which words such as *"Schicksal"* (fate) or *"Verhängnis"* (doom) exercise upon them. These are both words which are used as a matter of course in their scholarly writings and among the general public. They convey an untranslatable overtone of inevitability. They endow many Germans with the certainty of understanding the course of history in a deeper way than the more superficial peoples of the West. In this higher spirituality these Germans found a compensation for Germany's allegedly undeserved national misfortunes.

Hilaire Belloc, writing in 1902, was more indulgent. His "Germans" included French-speaking Swiss. "In all of them you find (it is not race, it is something much more than race, it is the type of culture) a dreaminess and a love of ease. In all of them you find music. . . . The German spirit is a marvel."

Not, however, to Nietzsche:

This nation has deliberately made itself stupid, for practically a thousand years: nowhere else are the two great European narcotics, alcohol and Christianity, so viciously abused. Lately even a third has been added, one which is capable by itself of completely obstructing all delicate and audacious flexibility of spirit: music, our constipated, constipating German music.—How much dreary heaviness, lameness, dampness, sloppiness, how much *beer* there is in the German intellect!

Many others had seen German life through a glass, darkly. At the Diet of Augsburg in 1518, Ulrich von Hutten said that he could recognize non-Germans because they stayed sober. Some twenty years later, Martin Luther deplored the "spirit of guzzling and swilling", and thought that "this perpetual thirst will be the bane of Germany until Judgement Day." Giordano Bruno declared that "drink-sodden Germany is the home of vulgar ambition, pretension, downright arrogance, brutal repression, petty tyranny, servility below and oppression above." Then he got a professorship at Wittenberg. When he left in 1588 he made amends. "Wisdom has built her dwelling here in Germany," he announced; "Divine, yes, divine is the spirit of this people."

Divine or not, its reputation continued unchanged. A seventeenth-century visitor from France complained that "to drink in Germany is to drink all the time". Just over three centuries later, in Prussia at least, they were still at it. "The Prussians," wrote Maurice Barrès, "are all under the influence of beer; it dulls them, soothes them, and sends them to sleep, it calms anger or passion, it makes them soft and forgetful." And, of course, it was accompanied by sausages. "Everything in Germany," Paul Claudel noted, "is a sausage – German phraseology, German politics, books of philology and science with their notes and references, all are sausages – including Goethe!"

Even German bedding has strengthened foreign prejudice:

In my bed-chamber, I found a straw pallet covered by a sheet; on it lay an eider-down quilt, a kind of large feather pillow, which in this country appears to serve in place of blankets. The maid-servant inquired the reason for my astonishment; and upon my explaining that I wished for a second sheet with which to cover my person, she found the notion so out of the ordinary that she could not contain her laughter. Had I not sent her about her business, she would doubtless be laughing yet.

This was a French tourist in 1821. At the end of the century, another was equally astonished:

The mattress consists of three or four square sections, which the idle chamber-maids put roughly in a line. The bed then forms a series of steps and inclined planes. Under one's head is a kind of sloping desk; the middle is flat, and one's feet tilt somewhat downwards.

Love, in these circumstances, looks difficult. Nor are they the only hazard. "German ladies eat too much and too often," declared an English woman visitor in 1881. "Big feet, big arms, big ears – these are three features you will find on any German woman," affirmed a French connoisseur six years later. Perhaps for this reason, they were regarded as easy conquests. "It is as if German women had different views of virtue from ours," claimed a further French investigator: "they are so ready and prompt to grant their favours." "It is the German women who do the marrying," concluded another. "If they did not make the overtures, over a cup of tea, most German men would remain lifelong virgins, between a brunette pipe and a *Stein* of blonde beer." It was a slight contradiction of Bismarck's boast that "the Teutonic race, our German race, is the virile principle that impregnates everything in Europe."

What truth, then, is there in the legends? Broadly, that some of the clichés still used about Germany date from a very different age. A few are as anachronistic as the descriptions of *Germania* by Tacitus so proudly quoted by nineteenth-century German nationalists, despite the fact that Tacitus had used his courageous, loyal, and freedom-loving "Germani" chiefly as an object-lesson to chide the decadence of Rome.

Early stories of German "barbarism" were partly coloured by memories of the tribal past; but they are explained also by the rustic, provincial, hierarchical nature of German society at the time. By the middle of the seventeenth century, the Thirty Years' War had left deep scars on the country; and not until the second half of the eighteenth did German philosophers, poets, dramatists, and musicians begin to be oustanding. Within eighty years, Germany had given Europe Kant, Goethe, Herder, Schiller, Haydn, and Beethoven. Then, in the nineteenth century, came the beginnings of industrialization. The *Zollverein* – in fact only the most successful of a series of customs unions – together with the railways made for economic unity even while the country remained politically divided; and other nations watched Germany's economy grow rather as in the 1960s and later they watched the dizzy growth of Japan. The Germans' reputation for hard work was partly a sign of jealousy. Finally, while their output was undoubtedly impressive, their intake of beer has often been exaggerated. Today, both Australians and Belgians rank higher in this particular league table; and recent surveys show that younger Germans drink more Coca-Cola than anyone else in Europe.

What does seem to be true in the German legend, however, is the quest for an identity. Without very firm national frontiers in either east or west, without political unity before Bismarck, and without an effective parliamentary system until Weimar and then the Federal Republic, Germans have always been in some sense characters in search of an author. This partly explains, perhaps, their feeling for flux and their concern for origins: in the nineteenth century, German philologists, archaeologists, and ethnologists were combing the past to find out who they were. Even today, Germany remains very various, and most generalizations about "the national character" are therefore doubly suspect. A ruddy-faced Hamburg sea-captain is very different from a stout Bavarian peasant, a Bonn professor from a scapegrace *Berliner*, a *gemütlich* Rhinelander from a Prussian aristocrat with a Polish name.

This is not to suggest that the stereotype offered by de Gaulle and others is totally irrelevant. Other nations, with other languages, can hardly help feeling that Germans live farther back in the caves of their being; that deeper emotions obscurely stir them; that German itself is a language for the dark pine-forests, full of shadows and strange powers. Nazi evil reinforced such feelings, but they were there already. It was partly the mistrust they created that helped to make Germany an Ishmael, and so paved the way for Hitler.

When Germany emerged from World War II, the search for an identity was crucial. One solution was to look backwards, beyond the cruel vulgarity of the Führer and his associates, to an older, more legitimate authority. Konrad Adenauer partly embodied it; but too many other landmarks had disappeared. Berlin and all it stood for were in ruins; there was no viable capital here. The old military, hierarchical ideals of loyalty, order, strength, and obedience had been fatally contaminated. Even German scholarship was not immune. Not all Germans, of course, were sensitive to the new situation: some found it too hard to live with the implications of collective guilt. At least twice in my own experience, in mixed European company, well-meaning, friendly middle-aged women have exclaimed with no trace of self-consciousness:

"Oh, I love your country – my husband and I were so happy there during the war." But the recent past could not always be exorcised, and its shadow stretched a long way back.

Research in the 1950s revealed that Germans still thought of themselves as hard-working, intelligent, brave, practical, and peace-loving – in that order. The British, Dutch, and Norwegians put "peace-loving" first among their own qualities, the French and Italians "intelligent". To this extent, the Germans subscribed to their own stereotype; and these years saw them working very hard indeed. This was one way of looking to the future. For some of them, it seemed to lie with the United States: countless young Germans at that time seemed to be wearing crew-cuts, bow-ties, or ivy-league jackets, and speaking English with semi-American accents. Even today, rebels against "the system" tend to wear the uniform of Berkeley, California. But for others, pure mimesis was impossible or unsatisfactory. They sought a new German identity as part of a united Europe; and as they did so their own stereotype began to change. Leisure once more became important. More and more foreign workpeople began to be recruited for jobs that Germans avoided; and people in the age-group between 16 and 24 began to show a majority preference for what sociologists have called "post-acquisitive values". The election and acceptance of a Social-Democratic Government led by Willy Brandt was a further landmark; but no less striking was the fact that all major parties now overtly pursued "social" and "democratic" goals. Even the German language has been rapidly changing, with British and American imports, especially into business terminology, but also – perhaps more significantly – a tendency for speech to be less formal and deferential, and even to adopt non-German word-order.

In all these ways, the clichés of the past are fading. Since most of them were very suitable to a rogues' gallery, this is no bad thing. Perhaps the last to go, in fact as in legend, will be the eccentricity of German beds; but the new popularity of *duvets* in Britain may be a sign that others are growing eccentric too.

Bel Paese

In a dull and dreary London winter, even duller, wetter and more dreary than usual, after having scarcely seen the sun for two consecutive hours for months together, it is a comfort to fall back upon the pleasures of memory, and retire in imagination to lands where a real sun shines upon translucent waters, and where cypresses and oleanders, gaunt aloes and trellised vines, are reflected upon the smooth surface of lakes which gently lap against the walls and towers that support them.

This was how a nineteenth-century English traveller introduced an essay on the Italian lakes. The modern tourist, flying into Fiumicino or Linate, avoids what once made Italy so dramatic for northern visitors: entering it through the mountains. To recover that sensation, he must go to somewhere like Angera, on the quieter side of Lake Maggiore. Here, the atmosphere of *I Promessi Sposi* still lingers. Along the lake runs a broad foreshore, shaded by trees at one end; on the slope running down to the reeds, fishing-nets and washing are spread out to dry. In the calm of the afternoon sunshine, the shuttered houses have an air of crumbling grandeur. From the balcony of one of them, a stone inscription says, Garibaldi once "harangued the populace". Behind them, the streets twist beneath high walls; on the other side is a view along the lake, down past the low hills to the plain of Lombardy. There ahead lies the land of vines and olives, golden in the sunlight beyond the Alps.

"Behind the mountains there are also people." The German proverb was self-evident, but long neglected. Older travellers to Italy came for the sights and the sunshine, not the people;

they picked over the Forum, and tried to imagine classical Rome behind the irrelevant swarm of its modern inhabitants. Arthur Hugh Clough, in *Amours de Voyage*, found the ruins "rubbishy" – but then went on to describe the doings of tourists: he too tended to ignore the Italians of his own day. For centuries, indeed, Italy suffered from comparisons – with its own Renaissance as much as with the Roman Empire.

For some, the Renaissance itself connoted Borgia ruthlessness and Machiavellian duplicity. In 1506, Albrecht Dürer wrote from Venice that Italians included "the most arrant rogues, the biggest liars, and the greatest thieves that I should ever have imagined to exist on earth." In 1570, Roger Ascham argued that it was "marvellous dangerous" for untutored young Englishmen to go and live among them:

Because, time was, when Italy and Rome have been, to the great good of us that now live, the best breeders and bringers up of the worthiest men, not only for wise speaking, but also for well doing in all civil affairs, that ever was in the world. But now, that time is gone, and though the place remain, yet the old and present manners do differ as far as black and white, as virtue and vice. Virtue once made that country mistress over all the world. Vice now maketh that country slave to them that before were glad to serve it. . . . For sin, by lust and vanity, hath and doth breed up everywhere common contempt of God's word, private contention in many families, open factions in every city. . . .

If you think we judge amiss, and write too sore against you, hear what the Italian saith of the Englishman, what the master reporteth of the scholar: who uttereth plainly, what is taught by him, and what learned by you, saying, *Englese italianato, è un diavolo incarnato*, that is to say, you remain men in shape and fashion, but become devils in life and condition.

John Webster's *The White Devil* and *The Duchess of Malfi*, with their crafty plotters, corrupt prelates, and ubiquitous fatal poisons, seemed to be confirmed by authentic tales of banditry and the Inquisition; and throughout the next two centuries the stereotype persisted. For Gothic-horror novelists of the late eighteenth and early nineteenth centuries, Italy was the unhappy-hunting-ground – the scene of not only *The Castle of Otranto*, but *The Castle of Rovigo*, *The Fatal Revenge*, *The Mysterious Florentine*, and so on. True, Mary Shelley set *Frankenstein* in Geneva, and Bram Stoker's later *Dracula* was from Transylvania; but Shelley himself complained in his letters that the Italians were swindlers and, all in all, "a miserable race".

This was the other side of the counterfeit coin. For those who admired their earlier virtues, latter-day Italians were a decadent breed. In the sixteenth century, Montaigne was one of the first to allude to Italian cowardice. "An Italian gentleman," he wrote,

once said this in my presence, to the disadvantage of his own nation: that the subtlety of the Italians and the liveliness of their fancy being so great, they foresaw from such a distance the dangers and accidents which might befall them, that in war they were often observed to seek safety before any peril was at hand.

This accusation was to be endemic, continuing well into World War II. "The modern Italian," declared an eighteenth-century writer, "is a poltroon." "Watch an Italian army march past," said Ernest Renan. "Their prancing and slouching is a mockery." "The military spirit in this country," concluded Hippolyte Taine, "has too long been extinct."

Vanity, however, was not. At the beginning of the seventeenth century, forty years after the end of the Franco-Spanish Wars and the "brain drain" they had hastened, the English traveller Fynes Morison complained that the Italians still

thincke themselves to have somuch understanding, and their Country to yealde somuch sweetenes, fruitfullness and such monuments of arts and fabricks, as they seldome or never travaile into forayne Kingdomes, but driven by some necessity ether to followe the warrs or to traffique abroad: this opinion that Italy doth afforde what can be seene or knowne in the world, makes them only have homebred wisdome and the prowde conceete of their owne witts.

Throughout the next hundred years, British visitors and on-lookers – especially Puritans – were disgusted not only by the ignorance, superstition, and sheer immorality that lurked, they thought, beneath Italy's decaying charm, but also by her absurd pretensions. In 1711, in the fifth number of the *Spectator*, Joseph Addison proclaimed that

the finest Writers among the Modern *Italians* express themselves in such a florid form of Words, and in such tedious Circumlocutions, as are used by none but Pedants in our own Country; and at the same time, fill their Writings with such poor Imaginations and Conceits, as our Youths are ashamed of, before they have been Two Years at the University.

Heinrich Heine, in 1828, came to the conclusion that "the whole of the Italian people is inwardly sick." "The fact is," added Felix Mendelssohn two years later, "that the people are mentally enervated and apathetic. They have a religion, which they do not believe; a Pope and a Government, which they ridicule; a brilliant and heroic past, which they disregard."

No less obnoxious than its pretentious decadence was Italy's insouciant filth. Goethe, who first went to Italy in 1786, did so both to escape from Weimar and to fulfil his longing for what he called "classic soil"; but he soon found that night soil was included:

The porticos and courtyards are filthy with ordure and this is taken completely for granted. The people always feel that they come first. The rich may be rich and build their palaces, the nobility may govern, but as soon as one of them builds a courtyard or a portico, the people use it for their needs, and their most urgent need is to relieve themselves as soon as possible of what they have partaken of as often as possible. Any man who objects to this must not play the gentleman, which means, he must not behave as though part of his residence was public property; he shuts his door and that is accepted. In public buildings the people would never dream of giving up their rights and that is what, throughout Italy, foreigners complain of.

They also complained, with Goethe, about the Italian love of noise. "The people shout," he said, "throw things, scuffle, laugh and sing all day long. The mild climate and cheap food make life easy for them. At night the singing and the music get even louder." It was still going on 150 years later. "Rome," wrote Philip Gibbs in 1934,

is the noisiest capital in Europe. The Italians like noise. It seems to give them an exhilaration of spirit. It is their way of expression, vitality, dynamic purpose, and the joy of life. The motor car has given them an easy means of indulging in this form of self-expression, and they make full use of it. Their motor horns have a strident and ear-piercing *timbre* not possessed by any other make of horn in any other country; and Italian drivers let forth its blasts without a pause, as they rush through the narrow streets.

D. H. Lawrence was one of the rare visitors who actually liked being driven by Italians. "These automobiles in Italy, he wrote, are splendid. They take the steep, looping roads so easily, they seem to run so naturally.... In the same way I always have a profound admiration for their driving — whether of a great omnibus or of a motor-car. It all seems so easy, as if the man were part of the car. There is none of that beastly grinding, uneasy feeling one has in the north. A car behaves like a smooth, live thing, sensibly." Later pedestrians have been less enthusiastic. One likened Italian drivers to charioteers in Roman races; another, from Germany, claimed that if Dante were alive today he would make Neapolitan traffic one of the features of Hell.

At least, it might be thought, the *brio* of Italian driving is a proof of quick wits: but Jean-François Revel, writing in the 1950s, dismissed this as an aural illusion:

One of the most popular clichés in touristic and literary sociology credits the Italians with vivacity, quick-wittedness, and sparkle. In fact, present-day Italians are among the dullest people I know, from the waitress or salesgirl who stands staring at you if you ask for anything out of the ordinary, to the university student and even the intellectuals, writers, critics, teachers, and so on, with their prolix, solemn style, a mixture of didacticism and disorder, and their lack of any sense of concision, allusion, or suggestion. . . .

Heavy and slow in thought, they are the same in their manners and their starchy politeness, with florid phraseology belied by conduct of unbelievable grossness; with great respect for the titles they lavish all day on each other—Dottore, Professore, Ingegnere, Avvocato. . . . (To acquire the title of Dottore, all one needs to do is pass the "Laurea" by submitting a "thesis", a sort of dissertation a hundred or two hundred pages long, copied out of various manuals. So all the typists in Italy, more or less, are "Dottoresse".) Finally, ineptitude and indifference as regards anything outside their routine. The legend that Italians are vivacious arises from the fact that as soon as they get together they shout very loud and all talk at once; while their admiring foreign audience generally fails to understand what they say. If it did, it would realize that the content of all this clamour in no way warrants so much agitation, and that the most piercing shrieks merely disguise the most banal and boring conversations.

Have Italians, then, any virtues at all? Yes, affirmed one German visitor in 1911: "A sense of form and sonority, of tone and colour, of proportion and beauty. A sense of beauty which in other nations is only given to exceptional beings, seems here to be characteristic of the whole nation." This was most recently echoed from the 1950s onwards. In the words of one marketing survey,

Typical of the Italians is their *buon gusto*, their artistic flair which in the past led to masterpieces of art, and nowadays is evident in the world of fashion and footwear, in car-body design, furniture, etc. The Italian buyer is perhaps not so much interested in the quality (or price) of a product, as in its outward appearance and novelty.

The Italians' fame as aesthetes is perhaps connected with another quality repeatedly praised – their closeness to Nature. Goethe noted it, although with some misgivings:

All I can say about the Italians is this: they are children of Nature, who, for all the pomp and circumstance of their religion and art, are not a whit different from what they would be if they were still living in forests and caves. What strikes any foreigner are the murders which happen every day....

D. H. Lawrence, in 1916, saw the same quality more sympathetically. "The Italian," he wrote, "is attractive, supple, and beautiful, because he worships the Godhead in the flesh. We envy him, we feel pale and insignificant beside him. Yet at the same time we feel superior to him, as if he were a child and we adult."

Ambivalence of this sort has long been common among northern visitors, charmed and slightly condescending, admiring the direct warmth and kindness of Italians' concern for individual people, but often amused at the contradictions it involves. Thomas Adolphus Trollope, eldest brother of the novelist, told a typical story in 1887. A cavalry platoon of the Austrian occupation army had been ordered to charge an angry crowd in Florence, when one of the horses slipped and fell:

The officer thought, "Now for trouble! that man will be killed to a certainty!" The crowd, who were filling the air with shouts of *"Morte! Abasso l'Austria! Morte agli Austriaci!"* crowded round the fallen trooper, while the officer tried to push forward to the spot. But when he got within earshot and could also see what was taking place, he saw the people immediately round the fallen man busily disengaging him from his horse. *"O poverino! Ti sei fatto male? Orsu, non sarà niente! Su! A cavallo, eh?"* And having helped the man to remount, they returned to their amusement of roaring *"Morte agli Austriaci!"*

Equally renowned is Italians' indulgence of their children. In *Sea and Sardinia*, D. H. Lawrence described another typical scene:

The baby, with weird faces, chews pieces of lemon: and drops them in the family cup: and fishes them out with a little sugar, and dribbles them across the table to her mouth, throws them away and reaches for a new sour piece. They all think it humorous and adorable. Arrives the milk, to be treated as another

loving-cup mingled with orange, lemon, sugar, tea, biscuit, choco-
late, and cake. Father, mother, and elder brother partake of
nothing, they haven't the stomach. But they are charmed, of
course, by the pretty pranks and messes of the infants. They have
extraordinarily amiable patience, and find the young ones a perpetual source of charming amusement. They look at one another,
the elder ones, and laugh and comment, while the two young
ones mix themselves and the table into a lemon-milk-orange-tea-
sugar-biscuit-cake-chocolate mess. This inordinately Italian amiable patience with their young monkeys is astonishing. It makes
the monkeys more monkey-like, and self-conscious incredibly,
so that a baby has all the tricks of a Babylonian harlot, making
eyes and trying new pranks. Till at last one sees the southern
Holy Family as an unholy triad of imbecility.

A rather wild conclusion from a characteristic meal.

Even wilder conclusions have been drawn about Italian
women. In 1765, when James Boswell left Geneva for Italy,
it was with high or perhaps low hopes. "My desire to
know the world," he said, "made me resolve to intrigue a
little while in Italy, where the women are so debauched that
they are hardly to be considered as moral agents, but as
inferior beings." He therefore besieged his hostesses with all
the urgency of a traveller whose post-chaise leaves at dawn.
Most of his hopes were thwarted; but other visitors since
Boswell have felt the same attraction. Heinrich Heine expressed it with the decorum of 1834:

I love those pale elegiac faces, whose great dark eyes express
such amorous melancholy; I love the tawny glow of those proud
throats, first loved by Phoebus and warmed by his kisses; I love
the nape of their necks, a little over-ripe, and dotted with purple
as if pecked by saucy sparrows; but most of all I love their
graceful easy walk, that silent music of the body, their limbs
moving in the softest rhythm, voluptuous, supple, with divine
shamelessness and lazy languor, yet always airily, poetically.

The male counterpart of these divinities was less attractive. D. H. Lawrence made the best case he could:

This is the soul of the Italian since the Renaissance. In the sunshine he basks asleep, gathering up a vintage into his veins which in the night-time he will distil into ecstatic sensual delight, the intense, white-cold ecstasy of darkness and moonlight, the raucous, cat-like, destructive enjoyment, the senses conscious and crying out in their consciousness in the pangs of the enjoyment, which has consumed the southern nation, perhaps all the Latin races, since the Renaissance.

At night and with their compatriots, this was all very well. In the daytime, directed at foreign tourists, it earned Italian men a reputation as predators that they have still not lost. Bayard Taylor, in 1859, was disgusted by what he called "the bourgeoisie of Florence":

No lady can walk alone in Florence without being grossly insulted, and even in a carriage, with a gentleman's protection, she must run the gauntlet of a thousand insolent starers. The faces of the youths express a precocious depravity, and the blear-eyed old men show in every wrinkle the records of a debauched and degraded life.

Hippolyte Taine, in Rome thirteen years later, told the same disgraceful story. "Note that this gallantry," he wrote, "is not very decent; on the contrary, it is singularly naïf or singularly crude. These same young people who will hang about for eighteen months beneath one window, living on dreams, will accost with words out of Rabelais any woman walking alone in the street." "Every male Italian," declared Jean-François Revel, "is, and cannot fail to be, obsessed by sex. In Italy, men spend their time turning round in the street to look at women's bottoms. . . . I doubt whether an Italian ever loved a woman for her face."

Is this why kissing in public has been suspect in Italy since the seventeenth century? As early as 1656, a French traveller reported that custom forbade a bride and groom to embrace when the priest had just married them. And as late as February 1953, the Italian courts were asked to decide whether kissing in the darkness of the cinema was "an obscene act".

Such are the images of Italy. In one form or another, most of them are still popular, even in Italy itself. Italians, like others, are influenced by foreigners' expectations – including those of some women tourists; in the mirror-maze of mutual contemplation, the feedback effect still works. This was borne out most strikingly in 1964, when Luigi Barzini published *The Italians*. Attempting to portray Italy from the inside, Barzini found that there were few native witnesses to be cited: "Descriptions of Italian habits and customs by Italian writers," he confessed, "are very rare and seldom explicit." Foreign authors were more forthcoming – which may partly explain why *The Italians* seemed to repeat rather than radically question many established ideas. "The Fatal Charm of Italy", "The Importance of Spectacle", "Illusion and Cagliostro", "Cola di Rienzo or the Obsession of Antiquity", "Realism and Guicciardini", "The Pursuit of Life", "The Power of the Family", "Sicily and the Mafia", "The Perennial Baroque" – many of its chapter-headings seemed to belong in the mirror-maze or the rogues' gallery themselves. Very subtly, indeed, Barzini seemed to be playing one of the stage roles assigned to Italians by foreigners throughout the centuries: here was the familiar cicerone, talking brilliantly and at great length about Italian showmanship, exemplifying with every gesture the qualities he described.

This very fact confirms some of them. Renaissance villainy has long since vanished; but with Florentine history familiar from his schooldays, any Italian businessman may very well see himself as a cynically "realist" Medici, and take some pride in being *"furbo"*. The Roman Church, again, may not be what it seemed to Renaissance Englishmen; but as a social force it remains very pervasive. Many Italians are unmilitary; some are vain of their elegance; some – especially in politics – use inflated language. Decadence? Dirt? These are more debatable; but noise is still the grossest national product, and Italian driving is still recklessly fast. Italian design needs little recommendation; nor does Italian spontaneity and personal warmth. The newspapers, finally, still feature many a *"scena boccaccesca"*; and any summer visitor will have seen the seductive undulations that enchanted Heine or the well-aimed glances that amused Revel.

But not all the legends should be taken at face value. Like those about "the Germans", they are partly a response to something else – economic or other rivalry, false expectations, a search for cautionary tales and object-lessons, or even, in some cases, simply a holiday mood. Englishmen's early suspicion of Renaissance Italy, for example, was fed not only by the religious disputes of the Reformation, but also, in the fifteenth century and later, by jealousy of the Italian luxury trade in clothes. Those who imported such finery were felt to be frivolous and unpatriotic; those who supplied them, decadent and immoral. Invidious comparisons were made with imperial Rome. New theories of character, based on climate, reinforced the image: a hot country made for hot blood and childish babble; love among the ruins was the deplorable result. Travellers, briefed beforehand, saw chiefly what they looked for. Renaissance painting had set up ideals of beauty: Tuscan landscapes embodied them, and so did large-eyed Italian girls. Rebellious puritans from the north, like D. H. Lawrence from Eastwood, Nottingham, found in Italy an exemplar of the deep organic awareness and physical immediacy that their own countrymen seemed to lack.

Concerns like these distorted foreign travellers' perceptions, leading some to ignore contradictory evidence and ambivalent facts. The Medici, for instance, were patrons as well as rulers, and that tradition has its modern counterparts: the Agnelli family, with a quarter of the shares in Fiat and a majority in Cinzano, also owns *La Stampa*, one of the best and most independent Italian newspapers. The Catholic Church of Pius IX and Pius XII was also that of Don Luigi Sturzo and John XXIII. "Unmilitary" Italy produced Garibaldi, "frivolous" Italy Marconi and Enrico Fermi. St Francis and Danilo Dolci belie its reputation for vanity; its supposedly florid writers include Dante and Leopardi.

If these examples mitigate the criticism, others qualify the

D

praise. For all their noise and apparent gaiety, Italians are haunted by sadness. It darkens not only their greatest poetry, but also much of their comedy, from Goldoni to Ermanno Olmi, from the *commedia dell'arte* to the late Totò. Nor is their aesthetic sense infallible: look at the modern bric-à-brac in almost any church. Or look at the outskirts of their cities; as Norman Douglas noted in 1921, "the average Italian townsman seems to have lost all sense of the beauty of rural existence": the Via Appia Nuova is as ugly an instance of rape by ribbon development as any in Britain or France. Even in Volterra, where alabaster is still carved in cavernous dusty workshops, its lovely translucence is often turned into bright Walt Disney figures. Are Italians children of Nature? "Naturalness," declared Jean-François Revel, "is what they most lack." Are they warm-hearted? "Future generations," argued Norman Douglas, "will hardly recognize the Italian race from our descriptions. A new type is being formed, cold and loveless, with all the divinity drained out of them." Their indulgence of children, so startling to D. H. Lawrence, no longer surprises Dr Spock's adherents – far from it: few British or American children would wear the spotless wedding-cake outfits that many Italian parents still impose. Finally, are Italians even sexy? Several of Alberto Moravia's heroes seem to be spiritually impotent; Italian Casanovas often resemble infants longing to be mothered; and many of their nubile girls soon turn into stout, domineering matrons. The Italian family, in fact, with its Mafia-like ramifications, is perhaps the only instance where the stereotype wholly tallies with the truth.

In other cases, in Italy as elsewhere, the clichés can be misleading. They are also the victims of change. Today, this is more so than ever; for what has long been notable in Italy is the process that might be called its gradual Milanization.

Milan is no great favourite with tourists. It rains too often; the streets are too ugly; the people hurry too much. "If Amsterdam is the Venice of the north," said one visitor,

"Milan must be the Brussels of the south." Other Italians, too, feel uneasy in its clipped, impatient atmosphere. Neapolitans envy its prosperity: until recently, the typical Milanese ate twice as much meat a year as the Italian average. Many Romans despise its commercialism; and their coolness is returned by the Milanese, who resent Rome's inroads on their taxes. "The Italian civil service," a Milanese businessman once told me, "is a form of disguised unemployment." Yet, like it or not, for more than a decade Milan has set a pattern for Italy's future. Against the old legend of the feckless Mediterranean, it asserts a new image – that of the ingenious young man in tinted glasses and a nylon raincoat, driving his Fiat along an *autostrada* flanked with advertisements for Agipgas. Against the ruins of Rome, Milan asserts the Pirelli building. Against stagnation, it asserts economic growth.

Milan, of course, is not the only focus. Turin, Bologna, and Genoa are close rivals; and under current modernization plans, dramatic changes are in progress further south. During the 1960s, Italy as a whole underwent its own "economic miracle". In that decade its annual growth-rate was more than 6 per cent – the highest in the Common Market; it compared with 2.6 per cent in Britain and 2.3 per cent in the United States. In 1959, Italy's average wages had been lower than Britain's; ten years later, they were already higher. Unevenly, but very rapidly, the Italian economy was being transformed.

Part of the price of change was social stress. Already in 1960, Luchino Visconti's film *Rocco e i suoi fratelli* portrayed the disorientation of a peasant family from Lucania cast adrift in the north. Already, Italian governments were trying to cope with the side-effects of "affluence" – regulating traffic, preparing laws against smog. All this reinforced the later protests of workpeople and students who wanted more from life than cars and motor-scooters. It also began to change, more slowly, some of the stereotypes so long cherished by visitors from abroad.

A nation that thrives on tourism has to be careful with its image. *Italia Nostra*, the private association set up to save not only Italy's countryside but also its threatened monumental treasures, including Venice, had long since used this argument. Now it began to carry more weight. Some local authorities have since been bold enough to attack Italian noise-making by banning juke-boxes; others, as in Capri, have banned transistor radios. In Rome, in the 1960s, the Ministry of Tourism and Spectacle even felt it necessary to launch what was ominously called "the offensive of the smile". It may take more than this to bring the national portrait out of the rogues' gallery; but at all events Italy, like Germany, is no longer living in the past.

French Polish

Here then is a portrait of the Frenchman: rationalist, devoted to the golden mean and the *génie latin*, prudent, conservative, given to the small-scale enterprise, distrustful of and incompetent at large-scale production, avoiding the depths and the mysteries, indeed, without a culture hero like Shakespeare or Dante, with only St Joan and Napoleon as inadequate, really rather superficial equivalents. This Frenchman is a realist, perhaps even a cynic, a hedonist, yet temperately so except perhaps in eating and love-making, capable of one kind of depth, that of sentimentality, politically unstable, hard to govern, apt to resist authority, yet in many ways devoted to *le droit*, an individualist, yet molded by history and society into a vigorous and cohesive patriotism, polite, yet capable of inconsiderate rudeness and indifference, devoted to humanitarian ideals, but not in practice a good humanitarian.

That rather lofty catalogue was published by the late Crane Brinton, formerly a professor at Harvard, in 1967 in a study of *The Americans and the French*. As an anthology of what many foreigners feel about France, it would be hard to better; but one of its main themes – contradictions in "the French character" – was far from new. Another American, David

Schoenbrun, had made the same point ten years earlier in *As France Goes*, a book that Brinton recommended. Quoting the army marching song "The French they are a funny race, parlez-vous", Schoenbrun had explained that "Most of the verses are unprintable." Still,

> Whatever the color of the words, the sentiment is the same; the French are incomprehensible to the foreigner, particularly to the American who is at first bewildered and then irritated by the contradictions of French behavior.
> A Frenchman is rarely seen drunk in public or in private but France has the highest rate of alcoholism in the world. Frenchmen are fervent patriots but they invest their money abroad. A French-man is thrifty to the point of miserliness in his private family affairs but will cheerfully raid the public Treasury and laugh at constantly mounting national deficits. A Frenchman prides him-self on his logic but turns off the heating system exactly on March 21, the first official day of spring, even though it might be snowing outside....

This too was plausible; but the same notion of the French as a bundle of contradictions had been put about thirty years earlier, in 1927, when Sisley Huddleston's classic *France and the French* was reissued in the "Travellers' Library" pocket edition. "The French," wrote Huddleston in the new Preface,

> are a people not easily understood by Anglo-Saxons. They are at once logical and romantic; they are intellectually curious and con-servative; they are idealistic and sceptical; they are patient and explosive; they are egalitarian and respectful of hierarchy; they are vivacious and industrious; they are vain and practical; they are brilliant and sober; and with all their love of play-acting and verbalism and the *panache*, they are, as we have seen since 1914, tenacious, serious, capable of imposing upon themselves an iron discipline.

Read that paragraph out of context, and it might apply equally to "the Germans", "the Italians", "the British", or even "the human species". Yet, once again, something rather like it had been said of the French fourteen years earlier – this time by Arnold Bennett in 1913. "There was everywhere," he wrote in *Paris Nights*, "a strange mixture of French industry (which is tremendous) and French nonchalance (which is charmingly awful). Virtue and wickedness were equally apparent and equally candid." Earlier still, in 1891, a character in George Meredith's *One of Our Conquerors* had uttered sentiments even closer to Huddleston's, Schoenbrun's, and Brinton's:

> As to the French people, they are the most mixed of any European nation; so they are packed with contrasts: they are full of sentiment, they are sharply logical; free-thinkers, devotees; affectionate, ferocious; frivolous, tenacious; the passion of the season operating like sun or moon on these qualities; and they can reach to ideality out of sensualism. Below your level, they're above it: —a paradox is at home with them!

One of Our Conquerors made many fanciful allusions to "national character". A few years earlier, in an essay entitled "Numbers", Matthew Arnold had elaborately identified "character" with "race". The first inhabitant of France, he declared, had been the Gaul,

> gay, sociable, quick of sentiment, quick of perception; apt, however, to be presumptuous and puffed up. Then came the Roman conquest, and from this we get a new personage, the Gallo-Latin, with the Gaulish qualities for a basis, but with Latin order, reason, lucidity, added, and also Latin sensuality. Finally, we have the Frankish conquest and the Frenchman. The Frenchman proper is the Gallo-Latin, with Frankish or Germanic qualities added and infused.

At a distance of twenty centuries, such clairvoyance about "the Gaul" seems uncanny.

To trace this tentative pedigree for Professor Brinton's portrait is not to suggest that one author copied another. Some half-buried memories may have emerged in their writing; but essentially these texts are outcrops of more general underlying attitudes. Some were based on actual observation; some were so neat as to seem rhetorical: but many were bound to be influenced by the continuing tradition they helped to keep alive. So it is that stereotypes harden; and none could be more popular than the legends about France.

Discounting Caesar's divided and superstitious Gauls, one of the oldest clichés is that of Gallic wit and loquacity. In the sixteenth century, an English observer told what he saw as a typical tale. A Frenchman on his death-bed was receiving the last sacrament; but when he was offered the Host he shook his head. "Forgive me," he told the priest; "but I never eat meat on a Friday." Frenchmen, the narrator concluded, would sacrifice their souls to a *bon mot*.

They were also notoriously talkative. "A Frenchman must always be talking," declared Dr Johnson, "whether he knows anything of the matter or not." Johanna Schopenhauer, the mother of the philosopher, fully agreed. "No Frenchman can stop chattering incessantly, even when he has nothing to say; in society, it is thought to be a breach of manners to be silent, even for a few minutes." Dr Johnson had compared this habit with that of the Englishman, who "is content to say nothing when he has nothing to say"; Madame de Staël contrasted it with the diffident silence of the Germans:

In France, there are so many readymade phrases on every subject, that with their help a fool can talk quite well for a time, and even briefly seem to be a wit. In Germany, an ignoramus would never dare give a confident judgement on anything.…

All classes in France feel the need to talk: speech is not only, as elsewhere, a means of communicating ideas, feeling, and business; it is an instrument played for enjoyment, and it enlivens the spirit as music does for some peoples, and strong liquor does for others.

"Nowhere," added a German lady visitor, Ida Kohl, in 1845, "does one meet so many male and female chatterboxes." Some forty years later, one of the characters in Meredith's *Up to Midnight* complained that "a Frenchman sees a dozen things to reply to before you have well begun: a *oui* or a *non* is quite enough to strike a new keynote for one of his symphonies, and he is not to be restrained." In 1922, however, Arnold

Bennett was more charitable. "I would hold," he said, "that the most important part of table manners is conversation, and there the French are finished artists while we are fumbling amateurs."

Still waters run deep – at least in English; and babbling brooks are shallow. Small wonder that the same Englishman who reported the death-bed witticism accused the French of inconstancy. They were quick to begin anything, but quicker still to abandon it; eager, but infirm of purpose; more likely to act than to reason why. That was in 1598. In 1626, when John Speed published his map of France, the accompanying commentary said that its inhabitants were "of a fiery spirit for the first onset in any action, but will soon flagge. They desire change of Fortunes and pass not greatly whether to better or worse." To an Italian traveller in the 1660s, their fickleness was obvious in their costume: "The French are slaves to fashion, which unites them in novelty and pleases their changing moods; they defer to it, insensibly, in everything." So great was its power upon them that "many Frenchmen eat poorly to be able to follow the latest mode". Just a century later, in 1766, Tobias Smollett faithfully repeated the same story. "They starve within doors," he wrote, "that they may have wherewithal to purchase fine cloaths, and appear dressed once a day in church, or on the rampart." These were the gentry of Boulogne – "vain, proud, poor, and slothful." Those who were richer were no less frivolous:

A Frenchman lays out his whole revenue upon taudry suits of cloaths, or in furnishing a magnificent *repas* of fifty or a hundred dishes, one-half of which are not eatable or intended to be eaten. His wardrobe goes to the *fripier*, his dishes to the dogs, and himself to the devil.

Close attention to fashion struck some observers as "feminine" – a quality that many attributed to the French for other reasons, especially in the nineteenth century. From Joan of Arc to Marianne, the French themselves have encouraged the impression: so has the gender of their country's name, made more obvious by its uncontracted definite article, which be-

comes a nondescript *l'* in front of *Italie, Allemagne,* or *Angleterre.* "For better or for worse," declared a writer in the
Fortnightly Review in 1888, "France has been and still is a
feminine nation: not effeminate or cowardly, but with a
preponderance in her of the vices and virtues of woman, from
the mother to the courtesan." George Saintsbury, in an essay
on Ernest Renan, spoke of "the softer and more feminine
nature" of the French people in general; while the *Contemporary Review* in 1898 argued that "their vanity is due to the
feminine qualities of their mind. . . . Whenever that impulsive
people becomes momentarily masculine, it resembles George
Eliot's Mrs Ployntz, and shows its virility in a feminine way."

French vanity and conceit are repeatedly frowned on. According to Oliver Goldsmith in 1762, they include the assumption that everyone else understands French:

An Englishman would not speak his native language in a
company of foreigners, where he was sure that none understood
him; a travelling Hottentot himself would be silent if acquainted
only with the language of his country; but a Frenchman shall
talk to you whether you understand his language or not; never
troubling his head whether you have learned French, still he
keeps up the conversation, fixes his eye full in your face, and
asks a thousand questions, which he answers himself, for want
of a more satisfactory reply.

But their civility to foreigners is not half so great as their
admiration of themselves. Everything that belongs to them and
their nation is great, magnificent beyond expression, quite romantic! every garden is a paradise, every hovel a palace, and
every woman an angel. They shut their eyes close, throw their
mouths wide open, and cry out in a rapture, "*Sacre!* what
beauty! *O Ciel!* what taste! *Mort de ma vie!* what grandeur!
was ever any people like ourselves? we are the nation of men,
and all the rest no better than two-legged barbarians."

Nearly a century later Arthur Schopenhauer – perhaps taking
after his mother – was equally severe. The French, he declared,
had too much regard for appearances. "It often shows itself
in the most senseless ambition, the most ridiculous national

vanity, and the most shameless boasting; but their pretensions are self-defeating, for they make them the laughing-stock of other countries, and have turned the title 'great nation' into a mocking nickname." Thackeray was no less scornful. "These people are so immensely conceited," he told the readers of *Punch*, "that they think the rest of Europe beneath them, and though they have invaded Spain, Italy, Russia, Germany, not one in ten thousand can ask for a piece of bread in the national language of the countries so conquered." Even Henry James, although a Francophile, could not evade the issue:

> Whether or not as a nation the French are more conceited than their neighbors is a question that may be left undecided; a very good case on this charge might be made out against every nation. But certainly France occasionally produces individuals who express the national conceit with a transcendent fatuity which is not elsewhere to be matched. . . . I don't know how it affects people who dislike French things to see their fantastic claims for their spiritual mission in the world, but it is extremely disagreeable for those who like them.

The "individual" in question – then – was Victor Hugo.

Next to vanity, the most notorious French failing is vice. Married women are especially suspect. A sixteenth-century English traveller remarked that with so loose a bridle, it was no wonder if they were sometimes saddled without their husbands' knowledge. This reputation has pursued them down the centuries, culminating in Flaubert's *Madame Bovary* and in Jean-Luc Godard's film *La Femme Mariée*, renamed by an indignant censor *Une Femme Mariée*. A typical British comment was that of one Albert Rhodes in 1885: "The Frenchwoman may sin against Heaven, but not against her credo of giving pleasure to men. She may be unfaithful to her matrimonial vows and drive her husband into an early grave by her infidelities, but she will do so with feminine order and grace." Her husband, however, may well have been just as wicked. A seventeenth-century Spanish observer noted that Frenchmen, "while they may have affection for one person, never cease to promise it to a hundred others." Smollett was more specific:

If a Frenchman is admitted into your family, and distinguished by repeated marks of your friendship and regard, the first return he makes for your civilities is to make love to your wife, if she is handsome; if not, to your sister, or daughter, or niece. If he suffers a repulse from your wife, or attempts in vain to debauch your sister, or your daughter, or your niece, he will, rather than not play the traitor with his gallantry, makes his addresses to your grandmother....

Heine, a few years later, alleged that "to vie for women's favours, to try to please and possess them, has been since the songs of the troubadours the single goal towards which a cultivated Frenchman feels driven by his nature and his senses". In this connection, even the French language was a lure: "to teach French to one's daughters," warned one German *paterfamilias*, "is to deliver them into prostitution."

Laurence Sterne, two years after Smollett, had tingled with sexual eagerness throughout his *Sentimental Journey*; and he set the tone for English visitors over the next century and a half. Thackeray in 1840 noted fairly soberly that "amongst the Parisians ... gallantry is so common as to create no remark, and to be considered as a matter of course.... A French gentleman thinks no more of proclaiming that he has a mistress than that he has a tailor." Arnold Bennett eighty years later praised the French for their lack of hypocrisy; but in both cases there was a sense of undue fascination. Bennett, in particular, seemed to smack his lips over

the spectacle of a fairly large mixed company talking freely about scabrous facts. Then for the first time I was eased from the strain of pretending in a mixed company that things are not what in fact they are. To listen to those women, and to watch them listening, was as staggering as it would have been to see them pick up red-hot irons in their feverish delicate hands. Their admission that they knew everything, that no corner of existence was dark enough to frighten them into speechlessness was the chief of their charms, then. It intensified their acute feminity.

Gay Paree, all absinthe and adultery, home of the *grisette*, the *petite amie*, the bedroom farce, and the can-can, had long been a playground for puritans on the loose: in the tacit mythology of tourism, it still is. It was not Oscar Wilde, but a certain Thomas Appleton, who first remarked that when good Americans died they went to Paris; Wilde merely added that when bad Americans died they went to America. But, good or bad, they still throng the buses that promise them "Paris by night".

Why they should might seem a mystery: by all accounts, French girls are frights:

I have seen all the beauties, and such—(I can't help making use of the coarse word), nauseous creatures! so fantastically absurd in their dress! so monstrously unnatural in their paints! their hair cut short, and curled round their faces, loaded with powder, that makes it look like white wool! and on their cheeks to their chins, unmercifully laid on, a shining red japan, that glistens in a most flaming manner, so that they seem to have no resemblance to human faces, and I am apt to believe took the first hint of their dress from a fair sheep newly ruddled.

So wrote Lady Mary Wortley Montagu in 1718. Smollett, half a century later, told the same story:

As for the *fard*, or *white*, with which their necks and shoulders are plaistered, it may be in some measure excusable, as their skins are naturally brown, or sallow; but the *rouge*, which is daubed on their faces, from the chin up to the eyes, without the least art or dexterity, not only destroys all distinction of features, but renders the aspect really frightful, or at best conveys nothing but ideas of disgust and aversion.

Nor was ugliness confined to ladies of fashion. In 1871, Bismarck declared: "I have travelled in France quite often, but I cannot recall ever meeting a good-looking peasant girl, even in peacetime; whereas I have fairly frequently seen appalling ugliness. There must be some pretty girls, though; doubtless they go to Paris to convert their assets into cash." Perhaps: but not according to another German observer, Dr Emil

Isenree. "The face of the Parisian woman," he decided, "rarely touches perfection. If the large nose gives it some distinction, this makes it closer to male than to female beauty." Sigmund Freud, of all people, agreed with him. "It would be hard to exaggerate the ugliness of Parisian women," he noted. "Not one passable face." And hardly one clean body, to judge by British strictures. In April 1864, *Fraser's Magazine* poured scorn on French washing arrangements: "a miniature basin, a water-jug no bigger than a coffee-pot, and a tooth-glass rarely used." And in 1899, when someone calling himself "A Brutal Saxon" tried to put *John Bull's Neighbour in her True Light*, he found that Frenchwomen were "the incarnation of un-cleanliness and sloth". Their underclothes were filthy, and the working classes seldom washed anything but their faces. The "Saxon" was silent about his methods of research.

With such companions, it was hardly surprising that men in France were thought to be obsessed by their bellies. Their reputation as drinkers was of long standing. "We can see, from the noses of many, what mash they prefer," wrote a sixteenth-century English traveller. For food, on the other hand, they were not always so famous. Smollett thought them gluttons:

If there were five hundred dishes at table, a Frenchman will eat of all of them, and then complain he has no appetite—this I have several times remarked. A friend of mine gained a consider-able wager upon an experiment of this kind; the *petit-maître* ate of fourteen different plates, besides the dessert, then disparaged the cook, declaring he was no better than a *marmiton*, or turnspit.

In the nineteenth century, however, they had a reputation for eating what Thackeray called "only soup, turnips, carrots, onions, and gruyère cheese". "Why do the French have re-course to sauces, stews, and other culinary disguisements?" he asked. "Because their meat is not good." This too was a long-established tale. Three centuries before, a Dutch writer had complained that all he was given to eat in Paris was herb salad. With so much grass in summer, he supposed that in winter the French ate hay.

Winter or summer, they have always been seen as individualists. "Let us praise the French!" exclaimed Heine. "They take care to satisfy man's two greatest needs: good cooking and civil liberty." But to nineteenth-century English observers, liberty in France seemed to come second to equality. Mrs Craik, once famous as the author of *John Halifax, Gentleman* – a novel arguing that merit, not birth, made true nobility, seemed surprised that the driver of her *diligence* thought himself the equal of his passengers. Another lady, Mrs P. G. Hamerton, herself of French birth, was still more struck when she asked a Burgundian peasant, "What's the name of this village, my good man?" – and he answered, "Alluze, my good woman." Henry James, in a Bourges café, was delighted to hear the waiter and the landlord call each other *"tu"*: it reminded him, he said, that France was a democracy. But this, as he found, had further implications:

The intensity of political discussions is sharper in France than it is anywhere else—which is the case, indeed, with every sort of difference of opinion. There are more camps and categories and "sets" than among the Anglo-Saxons, and the gulf which divides each group from every other is more hopelessly and fatally impassable.

As the English positivist James Cotter Morison put it, the French were as prone to form sects in politics as the British were in religion. This, thought some people, was why authoritarian rule in France seemed to alternate with anarchy – making it, in Freud's view, a nation of psychic epidemics and historical mass convulsions.

What caused this reluctance to compromise? In a recent Sorbonne thesis, a young French student of national stereotypes herself gave the answer: "Our intelligence." Matthew Arnold had observed a century earlier that

A Frenchman has, to a considerable degree, what one may call a conscience in intellectual matters; he has an active belief that there is a right and a wrong in them, that he is bound to honour and obey the right, that he is disgraced by cleaving to the wrong.

No wonder that Frenchmen were stubborn, and foreigners impatient. In 1957, at the height of the Algerian war, David Schoenbrun remarked: "The cult of intelligence is the very best and the very worst quality of the French." Some, indeed, might think that French clarity sometimes meant over-simplification; but as "the Cartesian spirit" it has long been an article of faith. In his classic study *The Character of Peoples*, André Siegfried emphasized it more than once:

You can get the last ounce out of a Frenchman only in the name of a principle. . . .

Our analytical spirit, our ability to generalize and our language, a precision tool, permit us to reason better than anyone else in the cause of reason. . . .

The Frenchman really believes with all his heart that there is a human truth which belongs to all men, that this truth can be grasped by men's intelligence, and that it can be expressed in words (at least with the aid of the French tongue). And for him—and this is essential—thought does not exist, cannot come into existence, unless it be expressed. . . .

Any thought whatever which passes through the filter of the French intellect receives order and clarity in consequence.

Siegfried's remarks may be further instances of French national pride; but others have echoed them. Henry James was pleased to note that

The good looks of the French working-people are to be found in their look of intelligence. These people, in Paris, strike me afresh as the cleverest, the most perceptive, and, intellectually speaking, the most human of their kind.

Was this an illusion based on appearances? Oliver Goldsmith, two centuries earlier, had remarked that

The first national peculiarity a traveller meets upon entering that kingdom is an odd sort of staring vivacity in every eye, not excepting even the children; the people, it seems, have got it into their heads, that they have more wit than others, and so stare, in order to look smart.

But many less mocking observers have agreed with Matthew

Arnold in discerning "a national bent towards the things of the mind, towards culture, towards clearness, correctness, and propriety in thinking and speaking". P. G. Hamerton, the husband of the lady already quoted, even pointed out that French peasants, however ignorant, were "at the same time full of intelligence".

And all Frenchmen, of course, are renowned for their peasant qualities: realism; suspicion, especially of foreigners; conservative caution; thrift; jealous independence. They believe this themselves, although sometimes invoking nobler comparisons. The novelist Paul Morand, quoted approvingly by André Siegfried, wrote in *Hiver caraïbe*:

> There is a striking resemblance between us and the Chinese: a passion for thrift, the knack of making things last and repairing them indefinitely, a genius for cooking, mistrust, traditional politeness, an inveterate hatred of foreigners, but passivity, conservatism interrupted by social tempests, a lack of public spirit, a great vitality amongst old people who have passed the age of sicknesses. Is the conclusion that all ancient civilizations resemble each other?

Havelock Ellis might not have agreed; but he was struck by French realism. French artists, he declared,

> are always serious. So far from wishing to avoid vital spots, it is at such points that they directly aim. All their skill is here; all their comic effect lies precisely in the surprise of audacity with which they succeed in penetrating to some intimate fact of life. Nor is this only in the sphere of sex, as our English minds brooding secretly on that subject are prone to think. It is so with all the vital facts, even with death, and the French artist can play daringly with disease and mutilation and death in a way impossible to the English artist. This seriousness—this precision and courage in finding the sensitive spots of life and penetrating deep —is reflected in the French artist's mastery of line, which in its precision and daring is the exact technical embodiment of the French moral spirit.

Realists tend to be wary; and many foreign commentators have described what a recent marketing survey called "the apparent mistrust (*méfiance*) often displayed by the Frenchman; he has been so trained to think for himself and rely on his own conclusions that he remains doubtful of another's capabilities or even motivation." Sir Denis Brogan even claimed to see this in the national anthem, in which "the French call on the citizens of the republic to take arms in its defence." "Caution," wrote an American historian, the late Professor Donald McKay,

seeps into almost every corner of French life. It is evident in the market place, where the average businessman is very reluctant to take risks even in the interests of greater profit: he prefers to operate in his cautious and traditional manner for a more modest —and, he believes, a more assured—income. In a world in which the characteristic business is family-owned, the fact that financial operations are closely scrutinized by those immediately interested has contributed further to this attitude of caution. This outlook has tended to inhibit the rapid industrialization of France.

"So," wrote Keyserling in 1928, "the most frivolous French-man is always at the same time a miser, greedier than the more calculating German." However, added another German eight years later, "the French like money not because of the power it brings, but because it gives them independence." He might almost have been predicting the policies of the Banque de France under General de Gaulle.

As this last example shows, not every cliché about France is a *canard*, wild or *enchaîné*. But several, as always, are inbred.

The most beguiling is the long-lived legend of French con-tradictions – the "and yet" formula used so often to show how odd and capricious the French people are. What in fact does it amount to? In many cases, merely an admission that some of the evidence belies the stereotype. "The French tend to be lean and wiry, and yet many French peasants are stocky and plump." "The French are a brown-eyed Latin race, and yet many Frenchmen have blue or grey eyes." *Canards* like these invented examples are sitting ducks; but many others long accepted are no less suspect. "The French are a highly intelligent people, and yet many still believe in necromancers and fortune-tellers." Applied to culture rather than biology, the "and yet" game becomes plausible: its only drawback, as a clue to "national character", is that similar games can be played elsewhere. Every individual is composed of conflicting elements, usually held in fairly stable tension; and most European nations are similarly mixed. So contradictions, as such, are to be expected everywhere, even in a comparatively uniform culture, where a number of national stereotypes can be found to tally with the facts.

That the French are talkative needs little proof. French education puts a premium on articulacy, and French society prizes wit. But whether the French talk more than other nations is less certain. To foreigners, the light, tripping quality of the spoken language, with its fairly even stresses and rather short syllables, gives the impression of a continuous stream. It seems all the more rapid if their own French is slow. But this is partly an illusion. Some young people in France are just as quiet and contemplative as their contemporaries in other countries: several French students who have hitched lifts with me have sat silent most of the way. Many of their elders subsist partly on ready-made phrases: "*Enfin, j'sais pas, moi, c'est comme ça, n'est-ce pas?*" or, in more bourgeois circles, "*Et puis, alors. . . .*" These fill gaps, give time to think, and hold the floor – as does the insistently hesitating "*euh*" or "*ö*" sound that many use as a conversational stop signal to ward off interruptions. A Frenchman's readiness to interrupt is disconcerting to anyone brought up to think it ill-mannered: so is his ability to induce a whole group of people to speak French with him, even when all the rest prefer English or German. But if interrupting seems arrogant, speaking French is often a mark of diffidence. Surveys have shown that the French are little better at foreign languages than the British. Taught to value clear expression, they feel even more shame wincing their way through English or sloshing through

German than the average Englishman galumphing along in French. Nor, finally, is their articulacy as unique as it seems. When the BBC was considering a radio programme in which listeners would ask questions by telephone and be transmitted "live", as has long been the practice in France, some feared that the British would prove shy and tongue-tied. Many months' experience of jammed switchboards and garrulous callers has proved the opposite: given the opportunity, the British are as talkative as the French.

Frivolous? Feminine? Obsessed by fashion? This can certainly be said of *haute couture*. But in other fields – in painting, in writing, in philosophy – it has seldom been true; and in so far as fashion in these subjects has any importance, its focus has now moved away from Paris. Nor has Parisian elegance ever been truly typical. Alongside the thin France of the intellectuals there has always been a fat and earthy France: for every Jean Cocteau there has always been at least one Jean Renoir.

French pride is another matter. Victor Hugo and General de Gaulle perhaps embodied it most powerfully; but it recurs, sublimely innocent, in many lesser performers. André Siegfried has already been quoted. Some of his remarks go further still:

When the human being is threatened, when the rights of the individual and the liberty of thought are in peril, men always turn to France, and there is always a Frenchman, whether his name is Voltaire or not, to champion the right of the oppressed. . . .
Among the peoples of Europe there is none which has gone further, I will not say with the fusion, but with what one can nevertheless call the synthesis of historical contributions from all points of the compass. Eighteen hundred years of history in an uninterrupted stream have made us into the most highly developed of the Western peoples and, as we have suggested, the most adult.

This was from a convinced internationalist; Frenchmen's belief in their own superiority runs deep. Nor is it always so explicit. In 1968 the British journalist John Ardagh published a study of contemporary France under the title *The New French Revolution*. Some of its judgments were severe; but in the book's French translation, *La France vue par un Anglais*, they emerged curiously muffled. "The French," Ardagh had written, "are accustomed by their education to a high degree of cultural spoon-feeding": the translator made this "a high level of intellectual nourishment". "In Paris," Ardagh had declared, "people often seem to lack the time or the self-discipline to be generous or fully human." The translator omitted the key words "or the self-discipline". "Civic self-help activities" became "*activités de type utilitaire*"; the French ability to be "rude, grasping, indifferent, and cruel" became "*grossiers, indifférents, voire cruels*". It was as if the translator – or his subconscious – were afraid of his public or unable to believe his eyes.

But even here some caution is needed. Much writing in French is less blunt and more elegant than in British or American English. The literary use of slang, by Louis-Ferdinand Céline or Raymond Queneau, has a quite different, more daring, racy, bathetic, and hence much funnier effect. And in the press, belletrist habits tend to mute opinion as well as to express it: mandarin delicacy of language shades off into hints and allusions: trenchancy is rare. Some years ago, the American novelist Mary McCarthy wrote a mildly critical account of one of Jean-Paul Sartre's political meetings, for a French paper of quite different political views. Although to an English or American reader her piece seemed reasonable, she was told that for a French audience it was "too strong". Against a background of such decorum, therefore, a direct translation of Ardagh's words might have seemed misplaced. As for the exaggerations of Victor Hugo, General de Gaulle, or even André Siegfried – to say nothing of such very different nationalists as Maurice Barrès and Charles Maurras, they have to be seen in their true context of deep political insecurity. After the seventeenth century – *le grand siècle* and the ardours of the Revolution, France had groped her way in and out of various constitutional régimes, finally stumbling into the disastrous war of 1870. The most bombastic writings of Victor Hugo and others reflected that humiliation. In World War 1, the country lost one-and-a-half million young men, more in proportion to her numbers than any other country; less than a generation later, she suffered defeat and occupation. André Siegfried's words a few years afterwards were partly a natural reaction, a form of whistling in the dark. At key moments in General de Gaulle's career, finally, he could have said with W. H. Auden, "All I have is a voice/ To undo the folded lie"; his stubborn pride was understandable when he saw so little other hope of redeeming his own idea of France.

One side-effect of de Gaulle's régime was to abate a little the legend of Gay Paree. Not content with cleaning Paris buildings, his Governments did their spasmodic best to purify the bookshops and the streets. The attempt was only patchily successful. The Olympia Press moved to "swinging London"; but others continued the battle against censorship; and although Madame Marthe Richard had long since closed the public brothels, private enterprise took their place. Today, there are still thought to be some 6,000 prostitutes at work in Paris – half the estimated total in France. In the rest of the country, indeed, the image of France as a land of licence had always been largely a figment of foreign imaginations: in the provinces, while language might be looser, conduct was as strict as in England, and the grip of the family probably rather tighter. What has really changed, however, as some Frenchmen only realized in May 1968, is the general climate everywhere. Although abortion is still illegal, and contraception limited, such remnants of Catholic influence are dwindling, and with them some of the savour of forbidden fruit. Such works as *The Sex-life of Robinson Crusoe* – a genuine title – seem less succulent in a world no longer so deprived. Recent revivals of the great Feydeau farces, *Un Fil à la patte*, *Le Dindon*, or *La Dame de chez Maxim*, have certainly packed Paris theatres, but more for their period charm and split-second timing than for any lingering "naughtiness" – a notion with little meaning for Frenchmen or even foreigners today.

Dirt in the true sense, however, is more of a problem. The latest survey shows that France is still short of bathrooms: only 55 per cent of French homes have them – fewer than in Switzerland, Britain, Sweden, Luxembourg, the Netherlands, West Germany, Denmark, and Norway, as well as even Portugal and Spain. Only 66 per cent have running hot water, compared with 91 per cent in Britain; and only 60 per cent have washing machines, against Britain's 66 per cent. Nearly half the households in France, moreover, still lack an inside lavatory. This partly reflects lingering rural backwardness; but the plumbing problem is also acute in Paris, some of whose cafés still have the most gruesome facilities known to man. Many, of course, have been modernized – but in some cases only with gleaming new versions of that tourist's nightmare, the swampy stand-up cubicle with raised porcelain footprints no doubt designed for a yeti. But Frenchmen, like tourists, are also sometimes fastidious. Alarmed by the old story that their water supplies are drunk several times before reaching the sea, they still shy away from tap-water, and drink about 2,000 million litres of bottled *eaux minérales* every year – more than anyone else in Europe. In this way, at least, they partly belie their legend.

Their fondness for strong drink is more consistent. Adults in France consume an annual average of 28 litres of pure alcohol – 40 per cent more than in Italy, twice as much as in Germany, three times as much as in Britain, the United States, and Belgium, and four times as much as in Sweden and Denmark. Seventy per cent of it they drink in the form of wine. There are altogether some two million French alcoholics: the highest proportion is in Brittany, closely followed by Normandy, the home of calvados; the lowest proportion is in Provence and the south. Only west Berlin has a higher death-rate from cirrhosis of the liver. But the gloomy picture is qualified by two faintly reassuring facts. One is that alcoholism correlates with poverty: a good regional policy could do much to remove its causes. The other is that among young people in France, whatever the drug situation, alcohol is rather out of fashion. Its typical victim is either an expense-account salesman or a rheum-eyed elderly smallholder with poor soil and access to a private still.

The legends about French food are a little harder to substantiate. One very ancient myth was exploded only recently, when a group of British livestock producers went to inspect French beef and lamb. On the hoof and off it, they were naïvely surprised to find it at least as good as their own. So much for Thackeray and his camouflage theory of French herbs and sauces. But some other stereotypes need qualification too. Certainly, France is still a paradise for gourmets, often in modest establishments: but many *relais routiers* are grossly overrated, and I have even been badly served in a famous Paris restaurant with three stars in the Michelin Guide. Certainly, French housewives are better equipped than their British cousins: they have more refrigerators, food-mixers, and pressure cookers. But French gas and electric stoves usually lack plate-racks, and some still have the grill inside the oven, making it impossible to use both at once. Certainly, the two-hour lunch break is still very common; but several firms, including some department stores in Paris, have introduced a British-style *"journée continue"*, with a short lunch-hour and a chance for some of the staff to go home earlier at night. One result has been a further proliferation of *"le quick-lunch"* and *"le snack"*. Together with convenience foods, relentlessly advertised on the commercial radio stations that serve France from Luxembourg and the Saar, these are beginning to taint many French palates. Even more sinister, at least for lovers of tradition, are attempts by British-style chain bakeries to oust the local *boulanger* by producing *bâtards* and other French specialities on an industrial scale. Opponents of British entry to the Common Market might find this grist to their mill.

Will France's notorious individualism be able to resist this trend? It seems rather unlikely, since only unity makes strength. And a glance at the French Left seems to confirm the legend. Time and again, warring factions make an uneasy electoral truce; time and again, they split apart on some point of doctrine, personal rivalry, or disputed tactics. And yet, however much Frenchmen themselves reaffirm that they are individualists, their unanimity itself is surely suspect. Even on the political Left, moreover, the stereotype is only partly true. One remarkable feature of the French Left is its steady support of the Communist party. Card-carrying party members now number fewer than 300,000; but even at its lowest ebb since World War II, in the elections of November 1958, the Communist party mustered 3,882,204 votes, or 18.9 per cent of the total. Normally, it collects some 5 million, or over 20 per cent. Some of these are certainly protest votes; and some Communist voters are certainly eccentric. One I know owns a large yacht and keeps horses for his children: another has a small madonna in a niche on the front of his house. But the party's doctrine remains collectivist; and if all Frenchmen were individualists it would hardly attract so large a following. The French state, too, would be a perpetual paradox. Do individualists carry identity cards? When an oil slick threatens their beaches, do they wait and call for Government measures, instead of fighting it – however anarchically – themselves? Frenchmen, in fact, have long put up with a centralized bureaucracy. In the past, this has helped to sap local initiative, and it may account for the lack of civic spirit of which foreigners complain. But it hardly seems a mark of individualism. Havelock Ellis, indeed, thought exactly the opposite:

That word "discipline" recurs again and again when we contemplate French art and French life. It is the special French moral secret, equally apart from the English spirit of self-reliance and the German secret of state organization.... The same spirit, the same disciplined instinct which subordinates self to a larger whole, is there today, manifested even in the smallest matters of life. It is to the French we owe the *queue*, with its cheerful recognition of the rights of others who come before oneself, and the Parisian workman at the barricades of 1848, who, when asked what he was fighting for, replied: *"Pour la solidarité humaine, Monsieur!"* bore witness that an idea, which to the people of most lands is a mere abstraction, is to the French mind a concrete and realized fact.

This is less absurd than it sounds. French drivers, in their nightly race round the Arc de Triomphe, may seem disorganized and selfish; but their metal ballet has its tacit rules and conventions, however fast the performance. Who but a disciplined people would wait so meekly behind the *portillons automatiques* that keep them off the *métro* platform when a train comes in? What but a sense of solidarity makes them so punctilious in holding open for those behind them the swing doors that block their exit? Legend has it, of course, that French queues are disorderly: but this, too, is partly misleading. Queue-jumping, in my experience, is slightly more frequent in London than in Paris – perhaps because some Londoners are too shy to protest.

Only at Paris bus-stops does the queuing system seem to fail; but here simple machines distribute numbered tickets – a minor but telling example of the French administration's careful logic. At times, it seems over-careful: the amount of paperwork involved in day-to-day contacts with the *préfecture* or the *mairie* is as great as the pedantry of some of those behind the counter. To pass a French driving test means not only handling a car to the examiner's satisfaction, but giving the precise official wording of what French road-signs mean. Yet ignorance of road-signs in Britain is one cause of accidents: so perhaps French logic makes sense. Where but in France, again, would a mother admonish her children to be "wise" or "reasonable" rather than to be "good"? Where else does education provide so fine a mental grid to impose on complex problems, enabling even the dullest to analyse them after a fashion, and to present the results in a clear and orderly way? Where else is verbal skill so general? Where else would an ordinary removal man, eyeing his client's multitudes of books, smile and ask him, "Isn't there just a touch of dilettantism in all that?" Obviously, French rationality can be overstressed. The same client's father-in-law, watching a herd of cattle pick its way past a queue of motorists, made the classic comment, "Very intelligent, these French cows." But no one who has negotiated with senior French officials, filled in a French income-tax return, or seen a film by Eric Rohmer, could ever plausibly argue that the stereotype of French intelligence was wholly false.

The "peasant" image, finally, is a little more complex. In many respects, the peasant past is still very much alive. Not till 1928 did townsmen in France begin to outnumber country-dwellers. Many of today's cantons follow boundaries that arose round eleventh-century castles; and village distrust of strangers has been thought to date from mediaeval fear that they might be carrying the plague. France saw no enclosure movement comparable to that in England; the French aristo-cracy, unlike the British, was not a mixture of nobles and bourgeois, but a caste which by the eighteenth century, in the words of one French historian, found it "unthinkable to live in one's château, lost amid one's peasants". The Industrial Revolution came a century later in France than in England; and alongside today's express motorways, some of which follow the dead-straight roads laid out by eighteenth-century *corvées royales*, there are still many farmers and small-holders with refreshingly conservative habits. Recently, one of them refused to sell a field to a famous exurbanite from Paris. "So long as I've got this bit of land," he explained, "I can still say '*Merde!*' to everyone."

Saying "*Merde!*" to everyone, and especially to the United States, has been a popular French pastime, practised most notably by the late General de Gaulle. It was natural, perhaps, to feel defensive about a huge, distant power on which France depended for her defence and sometimes her prosperity, but which pursued its own policies and spoke a regional variant of a foreign language. But the General's efforts to escape American preponderance were both national and essentially negative – leaving NATO, not fundamentally helping to streng-then and enlarge the EEC. Although he talked about Euro-

pean unity, he did much to delay it: by refusing strong
European institutions and blocking British entry to the
Common Market, he made it harder for Europeans collectively
to offset the power of the United States. In this respect,
Gaullist policy was that of a peasant ignoring the motorway
instead of banding together with his neighbours to change
its course. However, since the General's departure, French
defensiveness seems to have lessened. Charles de Gaulle's suspi-
ciousness has given way to Georges Pompidou's realism; but
both are supposedly "peasant" qualities, so the game of stereotypes will no doubt continue regardless of the actual facts.

While France may still be thought of as a "peasant"
country, far fewer Frenchmen could now be described as peasants. In 1906 nearly 9 million French people worked on the
land. By 1954 this figure had fallen to 5 million; and by 1969
it had reached 3 million, or 13.6 per cent of the working
population. By 1985, on some current estimates, it should
have dropped to well below a million. During the 1960s,
moreover, France had the highest industrial growth rate of all
the Common Market countries, nearly twice as great as that
of the United Kingdom. Already by 1966 the total value of its
gross national product, at market prices, had overtaken
Britain's; since then, it has steadily pulled ahead. Far more
significant today than France's "peasant" conservatism are
more recent signs of the times: the rising birth-rate and the
opening of the frontiers that have put an end to both bio-
logical and economic "Malthusianism"; the rapid growth of
the chemical, electrical, and other advanced industries; the
high-rise apartment blocks round Paris, and the modernization
of virtually "new towns" like Grenoble; the increasing numbers of technocratic "managers"; and the concomitant protest
movements that first notably exploded in May 1968.

Experience, then, confirms some French stereotypes; but
many are the products of circumstances now changed. As
France, like Italy, finds a new prosperity and becomes more
open to outside influence, so her supposed "national character"
is altering, for better or for worse. Foreign views of France,

and Frenchmen's ideas about themselves, alter much more slowly, since each image reflects its counterpart, and all have a life of their own. But what is already clear, and growing clearer, is how much the French, despite appearances, now have in common with the British. Both are proud and rather chauvinist peoples, conservative but reluctantly changing; once hierarchical societies with egalitarian doctrines, now facing radical challenge; once imperial powers enjoying world-wide influence, now overshadowed by the world's giants; once very sure of themselves and convinced of their purpose, now deeply self-critical and uneasy; once implicit believers in material progress, now obscurely dissatisfied and questioning its ultimate goal.

Yet, even now, stereotypes mask the similarities. France may be twenty miles from Britain, but in the other direction the distance still seems greater: the average Frenchman, like many continental Europeans, still tends to see Britain as an eccentric world apart.

Island Race

When I cross the Channel and arrive in London I always have the same feeling of being on a new planet.

This was the reaction of André Siegfried some twenty years ago. The British – often known as "the English" – have often puzzled the French, sometimes for the same spurious reason that the French puzzle the British: their supposedly unique contradictions. "Ten minutes by air from the continent," wrote one friendly Frenchman in 1959, "there lies a strange land."

Here the metric system is unknown, judges wear wigs, central heating is considered unwholesome, sardines are often eaten after the pudding, and the theatres are closed by law on Sundays. Nevertheless, the first jet plane was manufactured here, agriculture is more mechanized here than anywhere else and England may well be the first country to apply atomic energy to industry.

An almost religious respect for tradition does not prevent the English being highly progressive, and it is this combination of survival from the past and modern achievement, of prejudice and new ideas, of the static and the dynamic, which gives English life its special and often baffling quality.

Although this is a mirror image of what many foreigners have said about France, the British have always seemed eccentric, even to themselves. According to one recent Italian visitor,

the English like to be different. They delight in our astonishment at certain aspects of their way of life. One sometimes has the impression that their main occupation is to play at being English.

"The English," wrote the London correspondent of *Le Monde*, Henri Pierre, in 1969, "can never do things as others do, and even tend to boast of this desire to be different."

To others, "different" has sometimes meant "dishonest". "The English ... are good sailors," wrote Paul Hentzner in 1598, "and better pirates, cunning, treacherous, and thievish." As every French schoolboy knows, England is perfidious. The phrase *"la perfide Angleterre"*, later to become *"perfide Albion"*, may have been coined by Jacques Bénigne Bossuet in a sermon on New Year's Day, 1654; but it may already have been a cliché even then, since Madame de Sévigné referred in a letter to "that perfidious kingdom". Throughout the wars of the next two centuries, the same cry was repeated. French anti-semites even suggested that the British were descended from the lost tribes of Israel, and *ipso facto* not to be trusted. "Through the pores of an Englishman," wrote one of them, "sweats the Jew." Edmond de Goncourt thought that the British were individually gentlemen, but collectively thieves: he would have agreed with Bismarck that this was "their natural vice". Charles Maurras declared that "the spirit of the English is essentially that of Venice or Genoa in the Middle Ages"; and Henri Béraud admitted in 1935 that

I am one of those who think English friendship the cruellest present the gods can make to a people. When I see England, with the Bible in one hand and the Covenant in the other, upholding the cause of the weak or the principles of law, I cannot but believe that she is merely pursuing her private ends.

Even a professed friend of Britain, Paul Cohen-Portheim, in a book characteristically called *England, the Unknown Isle*, spoke of "English Cant and Hypocrisy": the capital letters were his. Hypocrisy, he thought, was only useful for curbing the beast in man:

It is just because the Englishman is a man of very strong impulses that his education aims at subduing them, and because the unregenerate savage within him is still pretty strong he keeps him chained up.

This view, expressed in 1930, had also had a long history. "Psychologically speaking," Keyserling had declared in 1928, "the Englishman is without any doubt closer to the animal than to the intellectualized European." A century earlier, Heinrich Heine had argued that "although he wears white linen and pays ready money, the Englishman is but a civilized barbarian in comparison with the Italian." Earlier still, in the same year that Bossuet had preached English perfidy, another French priest had called England an "inferno of demons and parricides, the home of a rabid but stupid northern people". Nor did the notion of English barbarism die an early death. In 1952, André Siegfried was still repeating it:

We Frenchmen, whether Latins or Mediterraneans, have more than a thousand years of history behind us. The Englishman cannot remotely equal this record, and in consequence he is nearer Nature than we are, which also means that he is nearer primitive barbarism. This gives him a certain spontaneity and freshness which we cannot match, but it also gives him a certain infantility, which we find very difficult to stomach. When I was an interpreter with the British Army during the first world war

I marvelled again and again at the infantile nature of the officers with whom I was associated—and in particular the generals!

Perfidy and barbarism are familiar enough reproaches; but the commonest of all is British insularity. This too dates back at least as far as the sixteenth century. In the year 1500 a Venetian visitor wrote:

The English are great lovers of themselves, and of everything belonging to them. They think that there are no other men than themselves, and no other world but England; and, whenever they see a handsome foreigner, they say he looks like an Englishman, and it is a great pity he should not be an Englishman: and whenever they partake of any delicacy with a foreigner, they ask him whether such a thing is made in his country.

Paul Hentzner, ninety-eight years later, told the same story in almost the same words:

If they see a foreigner, very well made or particularly handsome, they will say, "It is a pity he is not an Englishman."

Emanuel Swedenborg, the eighteenth-century Swedish scientist and theologian, said that they regarded foreigners "as one looking through a telescope from the top of a palace regards those who dwell or wander about out of the city." And J. H. Campe, a German teacher who visited England in the early 1800s, wrote that he was glad to reach Calais and find himself suddenly among refined, agreeable, sympathetic people, after having seen so many cold, unsympathetic, gloomy English faces, looking down on every foreigner with proud contempt. "They are very conscious of their advantageous position in history," said Ralph Waldo Emerson in 1856. "England is the lawgiver, the patron, the instructor, the ally. Compare the tone of the French and of the English press: the first querulous, captious, sensitive about English opinion; the English press is never timorous about French opinion, but arrogant and contemptuous." The typical Englishman, he continued, is intensely patriotic, for his country is so small. His confidence in the power and performance of his nation makes him provokingly incurious about other nations. He dislikes foreigners. . . .

When he adds epithets of praise, his climax is "so English"; and when he wishes to pay you the highest compliment, he says, I should not know you from an Englishman. France is, by its natural contrast, a kind of blackboard on which English character draws its own traits in chalk. This arrogance habitually exhibits itself in allusions to the French. I suppose that all men of English blood in America, Europe, or Asia, have a secret feeling of joy that they are not French natives. Mr Coleridge is said to have given public thanks to God, at the close of a lecture, that he had defended him from being able to utter a single sentence in the French language. I have found that Englishmen have such a good opinion of England, that the ordinary phrases, in all good society, of postponing or disparaging one's own things in talking with a stranger, are seriously mistaken by them for an insuppressible homage to the merits of their nation; and the New Yorker or Pennsylvanian who modestly laments the disadvantage of a new country, log-huts and savages, is surprised by the instant and unfeigned commiseration of the whole company, who plainly account all the world out of England a heap of rubbish.

"It is hardly to be expected," wrote another American, Price Collier, in 1909,

that having been so long dominant they should not be domineering. This expresses itself in the best Englishmen by an easy and natural attitude of confidence and repose; but in the second and third rate Englishman, by an attitude of provincial bumptiousness and impudence unequalled in the world. This is what has made the Englishman the most unpopular, one may say the most generally disliked, of men. . . .

He does not care for strangers, particularly foreigners, and he very seldom pretends to. Our enthusiastic and indiscriminating hospitality to foreigners, especially to Englishmen and Englishwomen, is simply looked upon by them as an acknowledgement of their superiority.

A Dutchman, Dr G. J. Renier, had the same impression twenty years later:

Apart from a relatively small minority, the English are convinced that they are, that they own, and that they produce, all that is best in the world. . . .

More amusing still is the cool conviction with which the English believe that foreigners share these assumptions. Every opinion uttered in an unguarded moment, every compliment deliberately paid with the well-known insincerity of the continental conversationalist, is lapped up and printed for the edification of the English reader.

According to G. W. Allport, the American psychologist, American soldiers stationed in Britain during World War II were found to dislike, among other things, the "conceit" of their hosts. For the Englishman, even now, still seems to a French observer "a Chauvinist at heart":

Whether in a sooty mining village or in a large country house, England remains the Great Mother, a mystical entity, a divinity whose name is not uttered. People say "this country".

As tourists, the British seem equally proud. "There are multitudes of rude young Englishmen," said Emerson, "who have the self-sufficiency and bluntness of their nation, and who, with their disdain of the rest of mankind, and with this indigestion and choler, have made the English traveller a proverb for uncomfortable and offensive manners." The Englishman, wrote a German onlooker twenty years later,

travels abroad like someone who owns the earth: he always feels himself English; never will he sacrifice his nature and his individuality to foreign ways.

In the 1930s, the Italian novelist Curzio Malaparte vividly portrayed the English tourists he saw arriving in France:

Pink and fair, the English disembark at Calais as if descending from a cloud. Dressed in soft warm wool, they walk among us as if clad in invisible armour: distant and smiling, the head slightly on one side, as if they were listening to high and far-off voices.

They were little different in Switzerland after World War II. In *This Way Please, eine heitere Anleitung zum richtigen*

E

Gebrauch der Engländer ("A cheerful Guide to the Proper Use of the English"), Theodor Haller explained that "many Englishmen are ashamed to show an interest in the countryside; they cross the whole of Switzerland with their nose in a newspaper or a detective novel; they travel, not to see what is happening on either side, but to get to Lucerne, Montreux, or Interlaken" – where they call for tea and toast.

Some visitors to Britain, on the other hand, felt that their hosts had at least one thing to be proud of. This was their care for comfort. At the end of the 1820s, Prince Hermann von Pückler-Muskau – "Pickling Mustard" to English wags of the period – praised "the extreme cleanliness of the houses" and was delighted by the armchairs in London clubs. Victor Hugo was more grudging:

The English have but one idea—to show off. They whiten the stone steps in front of their houses, whitewash their cottages, clean their windows, and put up embroidered curtains; but they have dirty sheets.

Not at all, said Bayard Taylor in 1859: "for *comfort* in domestic life we must look to England for an example."

True, we have inherited much from our Anglo-Saxon ancestry, but in later times there has been engrafted thereon a French love of show, as well as a barbaric fondness for glaring colors, which I cannot but consider as a retrograde movement. "Look at the Hotel of St. Dives!" cries an enthusiastic patriot; "nowhere will you find such immense mirrors, such carpets, such curtains, and such magnificent furniture!" Perhaps so: but when I enter the hotel, and (after my eyes have recovered from the dazzle of the gilding) look upon the curtains of orange damask, the carpet of crimson and white, sprinkled with monstrous flowers of blue, purple, and yellow, and the chairs of rosewood and scarlet silk, I remember, in grateful contrast, the home-like parlor in the London hotel, with its quiet green carpet, its easy chairs of green leather, its scrupulous neatness, and its air of comfort, taste, and repose.

"How thoroughly England is *groomed!*" exclaimed Oliver

Wendell Holmes a generation later. He enjoyed open fires: but many continentals were critical. Odette Keun, from Holland, complained in 1934 of "the windows that have to be left open, whatever the weather, so that the cold air can offset the asphyxia induced by smoke from the coal fire or by the fumes of the gas." Cold comfort was a very English concept.

Still more notorious are the rigours of English food.

Roasts! Boilings! Vegetables without seasoning, as if prepared for parrots! And poured all over that, sauces that the Borgias might have concocted: they take the roof off your mouth, and it would be no surprise to read on the bottle "For external use only".

This was a French visitor in 1901. "In the face of English food," wrote Paul Claudel seven years later, "there is only one thing to say: so be it." After a further year's experience he added: "English cooking isn't seasoned – it's anaesthetised." "The food provided here," said Price Collier,

is almost more than a first impression, it is a daily, thrice daily, bugbear.... The vegetables are few, and even they, as Heine— how Heine must have suffered in England—phrased it, "are boiled in water, and then put upon the table just as God made them!"

In 1957, in his novel *La Modification*, Michael Butor described what still seemed a typical English meal:

There was a little soup, a little fried fish, a few hard potatoes, and a bottle of red sauce on the table.... It ended with what was aptly named a "sponge" pudding, covered with that inescapable pale-yellow custard which leaves in the mouth a memory of paperhanger's paste.

The coffee that followed was likely to be even worse, unless it had changed since another French visitor's description in 1815:

A well-filled sugar-bowl, two cups, a very small milk-jug, half empty, and an enormous coffee-pot that in France would have been enough for eight: such were the contents of the tray placed before us. I remember a gourmet's having said that good coffee should have three qualities: it should be clear, strong, and hot. Pouring ours, I saw that it was cloudy and lukewarm, and I sniffed in vain for that odour of mocha which even the humblest coffee shares. At last, in some trepidation, I brought the cup to my lips; it was indeed no more than a tincture in which the taste of coffee could barely be recognized by anyone unaware of its presence.

Perhaps, as Karel Čapek argued,

the average cooking in the average hotel for the average Englishman explains to a large extent the English bleakness and taciturnity. Nobody can beam and warble while chewing pressed beef smeared with diabolical mustard. Nobody can exult aloud while unglueing from his teeth a quivering tapioca pudding. A man becomes terribly serious if he is given salmon bedaubed with pink dextrin; and if for breakfast, for lunch and for supper he has something which, when alive, is a fish, and in the melancholy condition of edibility is called fried sole; if three times a day he has soaked his stomach with a black brew of tea, and if he has drunk his fill of bleak light beer, if he has partaken of universal sauces, preserved vegetables, custard and mutton—well, he has perhaps exhausted all the bodily enjoyments of the average Englishman and he begins to comprehend his reticence, solemnity, and austere morals.

Certainly, the British have impressed many as heavy and sad. "The English take their pleasures sadly, after the fashion of their country," said the Duc de Sully, echoing Jean Froissart. The Abbé Le Blanc, in 1747, alleged that there were men and women in England whose families had not laughed for three generations. "I do not know that they have sadder brows than their neighbours of northern climates," wrote Emerson a century later. "They are sad by comparison with the singing and dancing nations: not sadder, but slow and staid, as finding their joys at home." But even Emerson was hard on British workmen:

Heavy fellows, steeped in beer and flesh-pots, they are hard of hearing and dim of sight. Their drowsy minds need to be flagellated by war and trade and politics and persecution. They cannot well read a principle, except by the light of faggots and of burning towns.

Nor were other Englishmen more lively. "A slow temperament makes them less rapid and ready than other countrymen, and has given occasion to the observation, that English wit comes afterwards – which the French denote as *esprit d'escalier*. . . . Then their eyes seem to be set at the bottom of a tunnel, and they affirm the one small fact they know, with the best faith in the world that nothing else exists." However, "a saving stupidity masks and protects their perception, as the curtain of the eagle's eye." The Englishman, said Price Collier, "is not intentionally, but constitutionally, stolid. His food and his climate have much to do with this." With reservations, André Siegfried made the same point:

In England it takes a real effort to get out of bed, and that is probably why the Englishman usually rises late, and why he is inclined to start the day with a solid breakfast. . . .

The English people are not well adapted to their climate, and this explains their special behaviour and reactions to their natural environment. The mediocrities succumb to a certain torpor and they go to sleep, while the men of energy resist these influences, and their capacities for energy are increased in the very act of resistance.

Energetic, perhaps; but silent, and even secretive: that reputation is at least two centuries old. "Their conversation? They have none," declared a French visitor to London in 1727. "They pass an hour without speaking, and have nothing to say but 'How do you do?'" Immanuel Kant thought that an Englishman would rather eat alone in his room than in the hotel restaurant, where the only extra cost was sociability. In 1817, one young French wit, Jean-Baptiste Defauconpret, remarked that to consult a barometer and to meet an Englishman amounted to much the same thing. "So far as I can judge," wrote Hippolyte Taine in 1872, "the English are incapable of enjoying conversation." It was the eighteenth-century German poet Novalis, otherwise Friedrich von Hardenberg, who first said that every Englishman, like England, was an island; but the remark is attributed also to Heine, and was adopted by Emerson:—

In short, every one of these islanders is an island himself, safe, tranquil, incommunicable. In a company of strangers, you would think him deaf: his eyes never wander from his table and newspaper. He is never betrayed into any curiosity or unbecoming emotion. They have all been trained in one severe school of manners, and never put off the harness. He does not give his hand. He does not let you meet his eye. It is almost an affront to look a man in the face, without being introduced. In mixed or in select companies they do not introduce persons; so that a presentation is a circumstance as valid as a contract. Introductions are sacraments. He withholds his name. At the hotel he is hardly willing to whisper it to the clerk at the book-office. If he gives you his private address on a card, it is like an avowal of friendship; and his bearing, on being introduced, is cold, even though he is seeking your acquaintance, and is studying how he shall serve you.

"Oh, these unmoving faces of a phlegmatic race!" exclaimed G. J. Renier; "... the perennial puzzle of an Englishman's face that guards the secret of a soul like a sphinx before a temple where mysterious rites are celebrated." "In this mysterious atmosphere of subdued personality," wrote a baffled French observer in 1959, "only those spelaeologists who fathom the dark realms of the subconscious can hope to obtain access to the English soul."

As if afraid of what may lurk within him, the Englishman of foreign legend takes refuge in the practical. In a favourite word, he is "pragmatic". The English, wrote Madame de Staël, "always seek immediate practical results." "They lack the gift of reflection," said Goethe: "disagreement and party spirit make peaceful reasoning impossible. But they are powerful men of action.... While the Germans ... torment themselves with philosophical problems, the English, with their great sense of the practical, make fun of us and conquer the world." Perhaps; but not without cost. "Instead of raising earth to heaven," wrote the Marquis de Custine in 1830, "they drag heaven down to earth." And Taine was even more scathing:

The inside of an Englishman's head may very fairly be compared to a Murray's Guide: a great many facts and few ideas; a quantity of precise and useful information; statistical summaries; numerous figures; detailed and reliable maps; short dry historical notes; practical and moral advice by way of preface; no overall view, and no literary graces: simply a stock of good authenticated documents, a convenient *vade-mecum* to enable one to travel alone.

The British, declared a Sorbonne professor, Émile Boutmy, in 1901, "feel instinctively ... that if they were to see all the various implications of their thought they would find it harder to go forward firmly, surely, and directly, to their practical goal." A German writer ten years later dismissed this as ignoble: "The grocer's mentality, which only appreciates whatever brings in a profit, is one of the English people's worst faults." It certainly seemed to make Englishmen conservative. As Emerson had noted,

They have difficulty in bringing their reason to act, and on all occasions use their memory first. As soon as they have rid themselves of some grievance, and settled the better practice, they make haste to fix it as a finality, and never wish to hear of alteration more.

Every Englishman is an embryonic chancellor. His instinct is to search for a precedent.

In this, Schopenhauer had argued, they were wise:

The British show their great intelligence, among other things, by remaining attached to their ancient institutions, customs, and usages, and in holding them sacred even at the risk of carrying this tenacity too far and making it ridiculous.

"They hate innovation," said Emerson. "All their statesmen learn the irresistibility of the tide of custom, and have invented many fine phrases to cover this slowness of perception, and prehensility of tail." He added: "There is a prose in certain Englishmen, which exceeds in wooden deadness all rivalry with other countrymen.... In this Gibraltar of propriety, mediocrity gets intrenched, and consolidated, and founded in adamant."

Among foreigners, English propriety was proverbial. For some, it might have been explained by the appearance of English women. "The women in England," said Stendhal, "are much taller than we are. They have bigger feet, and turn their toes out less; one can see that they walk for walking's sake." "Here," wrote Jules Vallès in London sixty years later, "the women march like soldiers; their bodies are too long, and they have stupid feet." Nietzsche echoed him: "Look how the most beautiful Englishwomen walk: no country in the world has finer ducks or turkeys." Moreover, they were badly dressed. "The Englishwoman," wrote a French journalist in 1874, "has no feminine instinct in her toilet, her pose, her gestures, or her attitude.... Once dressed, she is no longer a woman but a cathedral, not to be seduced but demolished." In this land of Amazons, an eighteenth-century Swiss visitor had observed, "the fathers, no less than the mothers, take the greatest care of their infant children. Nothing is more common, in the streets and public places, than to see men behaving like nurses and carrying children in their arms." Perhaps it was all part of the *camaraderie* between men and women that Taine thought so dangerous:

In the "middle class", intermediate between the gentry and those employed in manual labour, many a young girl allows herself singular liberties; for example, she will go to call upon the young man she fancies. On this point I have heard scabrous details at first hand.

"The idea of comradeship between the sexes," wrote Paul Cohen-Portheim in 1930, "is a very old one in England....

England is, further, the country in which the approximation
of the ideals of masculine and feminine beauty to each other,
which is now to be seen in all countries, first took place. . *shavis?*
In general, all emphasis on femininity belongs to the dim dark
ages, and man and wife often look so alike as to be in-
distinguishable." "The woman," wrote another French com-
mentator thirty years later,

is a companion, a friend. Men do not notice her, or if they do,
appear to pay no attention either to her clothes or to the trouble
she may have taken to look her best.

The well-worn phrase "How well you are looking!" can mean
equally "Hullo", "I do love you", or "She's looking like death".

But still more sinister, in foreign eyes, was the English blend
of sentimentality and repression. "The sentimentality of the
Englishman," wrote Paul Cohen-Portheim,

is perfectly honest, like a child's, and thoroughly in harmony
with his strong affection in real life for children, animals, gardens
and flowers—for the idyllic, in fact; and it is only reasonable that
it should gather greater strength the greater the contrast between
his ideal and the actual surroundings of his daily life grows. The
reason why sentimentality goes so well with a sense of humour is
that they are both weapons of defence against the tragic side of
life. . . .
    The Englishman has a tendency to ignore anything that might
upset his natural optimism if he cannot alter it; as he does not
want to have anything to do with it, he goes on as if it were
not there, not speaking of it himself and not letting other people
speak of it. This easily produces an effect of hypocrisy, and it is
hypocrisy in a certain sense; yet it is also one side of the instinct
of self-preservation. Thus it is impossible to get away from the
fact that sex plays a very important part in human life, but the
Englishman is determined that it shall not be publicly conspicu-
ous; so one no more talks about it than one talks of digestion
and other natural functions or devotes oneself to them in public.

"So much *froideur*," said a recent French observer, "risks
inviting every form of excess."

The English are all the more exposed to it because their emotive nature sometimes reacts badly to the pressures of their society and its taboos. In the case of weak minds or malformed characters, the reaction can be a strange mixture of perversity, cowardice, and thoroughgoing duplicity....

The attention with which the public follows the most scabrous news-stories—whose culmination in the courts is reported in full on several pages in the press—might pass for the simple curiosity of classical ballet-lovers watching a Voodoo spectacle; but it is difficult not to be astonished at the sight of a whole nation eager to know who the "headless man" was in a pornographic photograph produced in a famous ducal divorce case....

There is something troubled in all this, not so much a lack of maturity as a widespread malaise in the life of the senses.

Whatever their failings in this respect, the British have often been envied their political freedom. In the fifteenth century, Philippe de Commynes said: "Now, in my opinion, among all the sovereignties I know in the world, that in which the public good is best attended to, and the least violence exercised on the people, is that of England." "The English nation," wrote Voltaire,

is the only one on earth that has managed to regulate the power of kings by resisting them, and which by successive efforts has finally established this wise government where the sovereign, all-powerful to do good, has his hands tied if he wishes to do evil, where the nobility is great without insolence and without vassals, and where the people partake in government without confusion.

Montesquieu called England "the freest country in the world", and held that "if a man in England had as many enemies as hairs on his head, no harm would befall him." "In London," wrote Stendhal in 1817, "nothing military offends one's sight, and sentries are only where they have to be: at the royal palace and the Prince Regent's residence, the museum, and the bank." Hegel, a few years later, maintained that

The constitution of England consists only of private rights and privileges; the government is essentially administrative, that is to say, it cares for the interests of all classes and all estates of the realm; the Church, the communes, the counties, and the companies look after themselves, so that nowhere in fact has government less to do than in England.

"The Englishman," said Heine, "loves liberty like his wife; it is his possession, and although he treats it with no particular tenderness, he knows how to defend it if necessary like a man, and woe to the red-coated intruder into his bedchamber, whether he be sergeant or gallant. The Frenchman loves liberty as he loves his sweetheart; for her he burns and is consumed; he throws himself at her feet with the most extravagant vows; he fights to the death for her, and for her will commit a thousand follies. The German loves liberty as he loves his elderly grandmother."

With freedom go honesty, fair play, initiative, and courtesy – at least according to some. The British, said Emerson, "have a horror of adventurers in or out of Parliament. The ruling passion of Englishmen, in these days, is a terror of humbug. In the same proportion, they value honesty, stoutness, and adherence to your own. They like a man committed to his objects." "The people themselves have the root of orderliness and fair play in them," wrote Price Collier, who also noted "the enormous amount of unpaid and voluntary service to the State, and to one's neighbours, in England". Salvador de Madariaga regarded the level of public honesty in England as "singularly high"; the Dutch journalist J. H. Huizinga found the British "instinctively courteous"; and another Dutchman, writing in 1964, declared that "a blind man could cross London alone and never lack help." It was a far cry from Paul Hentzner's sixteenth-century pirates or Edmond de Goncourt's thieves.

How true are these foreign views of Britain? Since many are uncomplimentary, a diffident Englishman tends to believe them, like a hypochondriac reading a medical dictionary. Some are no doubt accurate, as others were until fairly recently: but some are certainly instances of folk-memory at work. Legends about Britain, as about other countries, have been handed down like family recipes from one generation of bad cooks to another.

The initial strangeness of Britain, to anyone coming from the continent, is not legend but fact. "How long have you been abroad?" The question, from polite but watchful customs officers, often seems to imply that going "abroad" is something special and even suspect, a mild escapade away from normality. "Abroad", it seems, is the undesirable country from whose bawds no traveller returns without contamination and possibly contraband: welcome back, a little warily, to the bosom of the family, to the castle, to the nest. Foreigners, facing these bulwarks used to complain of being interrogated by immigration officials: "How long are you planning to stay in this country? What are you coming here for?" Elsewhere in western Europe outside Portugal, such demands were unheard of; but the British authorities still seemed to regard the United Kingdom as a promised land second only to the United States: the patron saint of the Home Office appeared to be St Peter. This confirmed all sorts of national stereotypes, from British arrogance to continental excitability; but more recently matters have improved. The word "aliens" with its overtones of "lunatics" (*aliénés, alienati*) and of lesser breeds without the law, has long since vanished from the signboards. The customs have adopted the supermarket checkout system; and immigration officers are now said to be less forbidding – except to those with long hair or dark skins.

Even so, beyond the barriers Britain still seems a different world. Some Englishmen, alone in Europe, still wear big, hard, loaf-shaped black hats, with no apparent sense of incongruity. Most London buses are still huge red double-deckers, with a conductor walking round like a waiter instead of selling tickets at the entrance. London taxis are still specially built, square black vehicles with a very dim light to show when they are empty. Many policemen still wear largely nineteenth-century costume. Public-houses preserve their quaint distinction between "public" and "saloon" bars, neither of which usually serves coffee, is allowed to admit children, or is open at all during much of the day. British banks refuse to compete over opening hours, and are now closed on Saturdays; most shops drive customers away two-and-a-half hours earlier than in many continental countries; and many hotels stop serving breakfast at 9 or 9.30 a.m. Traffic still travels on the left of the road, but travellers on the Underground are asked to keep to the right in its subways; and even when at last adopting metric coinage the authorities introduced a fifty-penny piece which they announced as the only coin in history with "an equilateral heptagonal" shape.

At times, the British seem to delight in displaying the imperturbability made famous by the 1930s *Punch* cartoonist "Pont". A French friend, visiting London, foolishly tried to use his hotel wash-basin as a *bidet*: it collapsed and flooded the room. Guiltily, he rang the bell. The manager appeared, impassive: "Excuse me, Sir, you *are* a Frenchman? Ah, yes. The last time it was a French gentleman too."

Altogether, returning to Britain is rather like stepping into a British film or a mass demonstration of "The British Way and Purpose" that used to be expounded by the Army Bureau of Current Affairs. Watching some British television only intensifies the feeling. To be a placid, taciturn, pipe-smoking, tea-drinking, policeman-loving nation is one thing: to sit every evening, silently smoking one's pipe and drinking tea, watching actors do much the same while other actors impersonate lovable policemen seems to be carrying electronic narcissism to excess.

The legend of British perfidy is another matter. Although it lingers, especially in French national mythology, it was essentially a product of the past: the Hundred Years' War, the trial and burning of Joan of Arc, Anglo-French rivalry in the seventeenth century, the British conquest of Canada, the Fashoda incident, and countless other sore points. France's huge losses in World War I led to suspicions, from 1916 onwards, that Britain was not bearing her share of the burden; and in World War II the Dunkirk evacuation, a hair's-breadth escape for Britain and ultimately for the Allies, was seen by some Frenchmen as a betrayal. The Spitfire and Hurricane fighter aircraft of the Battle of Britain, they thought, should have been thrown into the battle of France. The Mers-el-Kebir naval action, the clash over Syria, and General de Gaulle's exclusion from the landings in North Africa – all these heightened French mistrust. After World War II, Britain's slow hesitation waltz with European unity for a long time confirmed the stereotype: no wonder some Gaullists still believe that she will pervert the Common Market for her own ends. Is all this suspicion justified? Perhaps the best answer was given long ago by an Austrian Ambassador in London:

Most of the British Ministers and politicians are far more ignorant, inexact, and amateurish than we believe. A good deal that we interpret as deceit is in fact merely the result of ignorance and superficiality and is due to carelessness and confusion.

The charge of British "barbarism" is easier to refute. Perhaps it springs from the bluntness, already noted, of much British writing and speaking; perhaps it was associated with the image of John Bull. Undoubtedly, some British people lack the finesse on which some French people pride themselves: but there are brutes and dandies in every nation. Those Frenchmen who believe themselves unique as the heirs to "more than a thousand years of history" might look more closely at the seventh-century Anglo-Saxon masterpieces found in the Sutton Hoo burial, or the glowing, sophisticated art of the Lindisfarne Gospels. The difference, if any, lies not in the age of the respective societies, but in the emphasis each lays on "civilized" pursuits. Here, there seems no reason to think the British outstanding, but even less to allege that they lag behind.

The British love of comfort, on the other hand, is too well attested to be mythical. An Englishman abroad, for example, finds it hard to buy a really comfortable armchair. If he finds one, it will often be described as "an English *club*". Continental upholsterers, it seems, still see Britain as a Wodehousian land of gentleman's clubs where peers, statesmen, bishops, and learned professors doze behind *The Times* or *Country Life* in vast leather armchairs in front of a blazing grate. For their own countrymen they provide less welcoming substitutes – either upright *bergères* with hard satin seats and padded wooden arms, or pieces of airport furniture evidently designed for Statistical Man. To this extent, the stereotype is valid. But ever since central heating became widespread on the continent, the legend of British comfort has been tarnished, and foreign dislike of British draughts has grown. "Doesn't central heating make you soft?" asked one British family in the 1950s. By the later 1960s, they and many others had installed it; so the once discredited cliché may again be coming true.

The legend of British food is also changing. Schools, most universities, and – of all places – hospitals still seem to practise culinary archaeology, unearthing ancient dishes of soggy cabbage, grey boiled potatoes, leather meat, prison gravy, pudding, and chemical custard; but feats like these are increasingly rare. If anything, some people now seem obsessed by their taste-buds. Good food guides have made a cult of unbottled mayonnaise and unprofessional pâté: they write about cooking with butter as if cholesterol were a seaside resort in Spain. But together with foreign travel and Chinese immigration, they have helped to bury the old beef-and-beer image of cooking in Britain, if not yet all the horrors of Michel Butor's memorable meal. At least one Frenchman I know now comes to London to eat as well as to shop. So much has the picture changed, in fact, that an oppositite stereotype may even be emerging. Some opponents of British entry to the Common Market seemed to believe that Britain was better fed than its six founder-members – although, in reality, their citizens consume a daily average of slightly more protein, slightly less carbohydrate, and very much less fat. In this connection, a Dutch *au pair* girl tells a revealing story:

I remember one lunch-time when the family I was staying with were eating tomatoes. The grandfather commented on how tasty they were, and how much better English food was compared to foreign. When we had finished eating I mentioned that the tomatoes were Italian, not English. For a while there was silence until the grandfather complained that he was not feeling well. He said it was probably the tomatoes, and went to bed.

Another *au pair* girl, from Germany, contradicts the legend that the British are heavy and sad. "What I do like about the English," she told an interviewer, "is that people are more carefree." She was referring to the current tolerance of eccentricity. "If you want to wear different clothes and make-up to everybody else you can do so and nobody bothers you." But "carefree" also describes the change of style that marked the 1960s. A decade earlier, the impression of visiting a film-set when coming to London was especially strong. It might have been an Ealing comedy or a Hollywood picture of British life like Ernst Lubitsch's *Cluny Brown*. There was the same feeling of playfulness, blending Emett, Ronald Searle, and Joyce Grenfell; the same air of reviving some pre-war pageant, all busbies and beefeaters, nannies and commissionaires. Some of the young men of the 1950s, in particular, seemed consciously anachronistic, sporting furled umbrellas, British Warms, and Edwardian suits with camel-hair waistcoats and striped shirts. It was as if, not knowing what style to call their own, they had opted for that of their grandfathers. Then, ten years later, the city of carriage lamps and Georgian terraces became what journalists called "swinging London", and Carnaby Street eclipsed Savile Row.

Whether it was more than a surface change is an open question. The heavy sobriety described by nineteenth-century visitors was partly a facet of hard-working Victorian Britain, then deeply involved in social and economic turmoil. Perhaps many people were simply tired. Today the pace is no less hectic; and despite London's livelier décor, many of its inhabitants seem to be withdrawn as if for self-protection, or even in a few cases almost clinically depressed. However, this

need for escape or psychological armour is now universal:
the strains of overcrowding and rush-hours are much the same
in any big city, whether London, New York, or Paris. A
necessarily subjective comparison of faces in the Underground, the Subway, and the *métro* suggests that in this
respect, at least, Britain is no longer unique.

What helped to reinforce its "heavy" image was the habit
of silence or slow, laconic speech. Visitors are still struck by
it. The British, said one *au pair* girl,

are reserved and can be extremely difficult to get to know. In
the Netherlands, if I introduced you to my friends they would
immediately begin asking you questions. In London, it is different. When I am introduced to people they just say hello, and
that's it, no more.

"English people," said a girl from Paris, "don't come up and
talk to you like other nationalities do." "English people are
very reserved, I find," said an Italian girl,

On the Underground they keep their heads buried in their
newspapers and books, and don't talk to each other. In Italy, if a
train stops at a station for a while, everybody talks. The family
I am with at the moment are very kind, but it took several days
before they all started speaking freely to me.

A survey conducted among young visitors to Britain in 1962
showed that 24 per cent began by believing the British to be
distant, reserved, and unsociable, while only 15 per cent
initially thought them kind, friendly, nice, polite, hospitable,
and helpful. After some time in the country, 55 per cent found
the British friendly, helpful, etc.; but 37 per cent still considered them "insincere, false, too polite to speak the truth,
hypocrites, and without feeling", or believed that it was
"often impossible to know what they are feeling or thinking".

But even this impression, encouraged as it was by public-
school training, was always partly illusory. "The legend that
the English people are a cold and restrained race, modest and
self-effacing, immobile of feature and averse from emotional
display," wrote St John Ervine in 1934, "is entirely false. Only

a small, intensely self-conscious and rather smug section of
the English people in a brief period of their history have been
addicted to good form, that frozen-faced affectation of imperturbability which is more proper to a person who spends
the greater part of his time in playing poker than to one who
has general human habits. The working people of England
have always been cheerful, gay, and hilarious." Odette
Keun, in the same year, explained that

> The Englishman exasperates us chiefly because he does not like
> to explain. This constitutional antipathy for spontaneous, con-
> tinual and definite articulateness drives us in irritation to indict
> him for stupidity.

And G. J. Renier a few years earlier had delighted in the
subtleties of English conversation:

> The Englishman is a being of delicate shades and distinctions.
> Behind his serene face and reserved manner, he hides the reactions
> of an appreciative mind. He may not utter them directly, but he
> loves to pour himself out by implication. Oh, the strange charm
> of two English people seeking one another, and finding one
> another through the barrier of conventional talk! No brutal
> searchlight, as between continentals, to set out the other person
> in clear-cut outline. There is a pleasant game without set rules,
> thoughts are thrown out that dance like fairies on the thrilling
> air of a hot summer's noon, meeting and joining hands for a
> dance that defies the laws of gravity. An allusion to a half-
> forgotten admission, a hint that is thrown out, caught up with-
> out seeming effort, memories that rustle, dulled chords that
> faintly vibrate. Echoes re-echo, minds open and admit a new
> notion which is silently stored up. It is the greatest and finest
> game the English play—and do they even know that it exists?
> Yet the social results of this game are endless. It has done
> more than many obvious and material factors to shape the mode
> in which the English have finally arranged to live together. Ad-
> mittedly as among southerners, fatally and unavowedly as in
> England, conversation is what holds people together each time
> they suspend their function as *Homo oeconomicus*. But in this
> country the spoken word plays so small a part in conversation,
> while the depths of reminiscence, of common mental possession

on which conversation relies are so important, that the prerequisite for its success must of necessity be common to few people only. Introduce a stranger, and he floats on the oily surface. He does not share the great adventure of diving into the common fund. Each class, each circle within its own class is cut off from every other. Outside each charmed circle, the language of implication loses its meaning.

Renier, however, was not always right. He built part of his theory of English pragmatism on a friend's remark, "I am afraid we have no telephone":

> My friend meant not fear, but uncertainty. As far as he could guarantee, there was no telephone in the house. But he had been out. On coming home, we had walked at once into his study. We had not explored the living-room, nor the dining-room, nor any of the other closets and apartments. A kind Postmaster-General might have installed the telephone in his absence. This was what my friend meant: "I cannot state with finality that we have no telephone, but, so far as my imperfect realization of a world which we can only know through experience goes—we have no telephone."

What the friend meant, of course, was nothing of the kind: "I'm afraid" was simply an apology. If this is a reminder to treat stereotypes – and theorizing – with caution, it still need not invalidate the idea that the British are pragmatic. One of the faults in British policy-making may be precisely that. As Andrew Shonfield has put it,

> There is, even among reformers, an established penchant for the piecemeal.... It is as if the British political genius were entirely devoted to the business of make-do and mend.

Harold Wilson's memoir of his years as British Prime Minister partly corroborates this remark. To judge from his narrative, crisis succeeded crisis with only the briefest respite. The balance of payments was a constant preoccupation: little attention could be spared for steady long-term goals. This may be the fate of any modern British government; it implies no special weakness on the Left. The extreme Left, indeed, has always been more doctrinaire than pragmatic; and Dean Acheson's stinging remark that Britain had lost an Empire but not yet found a role was made on December 5, 1962, after a full decade of Conservative power. It was a Conservative government at that time, moreover, which saw no inconsistency in concluding the Nassau Polaris agreement with the United States while trying to persuade de Gaulle to let Britain join the Common Market. So ingrained are pragmatic habits that either civil servants or their masters seem to have forgotten E. M. Forster's advice, "Only connect."

Are the British, as many observers think, a deeply conservative people? One reason why they seemed so in the nineteenth century was precisely that, like the present, it was a time of rapid change. With so much innovation going on all round them – with farmers barely recovering from the repeal of the Corn Laws; with railways carving their way through the countryside; with factories and factory towns springing up like ugly mushrooms; with medicine swelling the population; and with new political demands bursting the administrative system – it was natural to cling to familiar forms in unimportant matters, and disguise radical change with conservative dress. Similar reflexes were at work in the nineteen-fifties, as has been suggested. Harold Macmillan's Edwardian style contrasted sharply with his "wind of change" policy in Africa and his espousal of the Common Market: his archaic camouflage was a sop to human nature, perhaps as wilfully misleading as De Gaulle's reassurance of the Algiers settlers, *"Je vous ai compris"*. On the Common Market it was self-defeating, since Britain's cautious movement into Europe was slow enough to make possible the Gaullist veto of January 1963. But whatever the style and its spillover, there seems no basic reason to believe that the British are more conservative than other nations. Havelock Ellis thought quite the opposite:

The English have always been great amateurs, not only in art but in science, even in life itself. That is the natural method of the individualist. It involves the spirit of adventure, a love of risk, a fine relish for the unknown, an immense self-reliance, and the caution, the diffidence, the perpetual self-questioning without which all the other qualities would merely point the road to destruction. Schools, universities, even traditions have played a comparatively small part in the production of English genius. Everywhere we see pioneers setting out, often alone and unaided, hampered by difficulties on all sides, for the conquest of some new world. The type of the men of this race—the remark has been made before—is set forth in the one English novel which belongs to universal literature. Robinson Crusoe is the complete Englishman. A supreme amateur, cheerfully facing immense difficulties, endlessly versatile in aptitude and resource, joyously exploring a new earth and patiently building up a new civilization from the simplest and most unpromising materials, Robinson Crusoe is the type of every Englishman who has sailed to find the Poles or penetrated the heart of Africa, ruled provinces in India or founded colonies in Australia or painfully sought out the secrets of Nature. Isaac Newton or Charles Darwin, the Englishman is still Robinson Crusoe.

That fine piece of British mythology dates from 1916. Today, the cult of the amateur looks much more suspect; and Robinson Crusoe seems the perfect exemplar of insularity. But it would be sad – and inaccurate – to think that no such spirit survived.

The sex life of Robinson Crusoe, despite later pornographic literature, was certainly restricted; but foreign views of British propriety are rather restricted too. Self-control in general is undoubtedly a prized British virtue: in an Anglo-American survey conducted in 1951, 30 per cent of the English respondents rated it highly, as against only 8 per cent of the Americans. But from the eighteenth century to the passing of the Street Offences Act in 1959, visitors continually gaped at the armies of London prostitutes, whom Pückler-Muskau called "those unhappy women with whom London swarms". Today, with greater prosperity and more amateur competitors, their profession is said to be shrinking; but whereas British reticence was once a byword, such puritan excess seems almost to have turned to its opposite. For some, the breaking of nursery taboos has become virtually an obsession; but for others, concern with physical love is in part a quest for something more general. The bedroom, now, is one of the few places where we are sharply reminded both of our status as human animals rather than voters, and of our humble equality and defencelessness. As John Middleton Murry wrote in 1957, "Our demand on marriage is become so great because in the world in which we live all other social relations are become so impersonal and dehumanized."

Is this a sign of what Paul Cohen-Portheim called "sentimentality"? Perhaps it is; but in French the word's connotations are slightly less severe. Many foreign observers have been charmed, as well as surprised, by British domesticity, love of animals, and care for homes and gardens. "England," said Oliver Wendell Holmes, "is the paradise of horses." G. J. Renier declared that "As England's grass is greenest, so its animals are the happiest in the world." Whether this be true or not at a time when the Royal Society for the Prevention of Cruelty to Animals is appealing for funds and urging people not to abandon pets bought in haste and regretted at leisure, the English love of animals is hard to eradicate, not least from continental mythology.

Equally deep-rooted is the British love of home. Perhaps, nowadays, this is not quite unique. With the growth of prosperity, more and more flat-dwelling Frenchmen have been able to invest in weekend cottages. Germans, who already had the habit, have done likewise; and as Italy's economy continues to grow, more Italians may come to do the same. Very gradually, with full employment, do-it-yourself is becoming more widespread in Germany and France. But despite this, and despite British slums and housing shortages, Britain remains the land of domesticity *par excellence*. Only 13 per cent of the British live in flats, compared with 68 per cent of the Germans, 56 per cent of the Italians, and 38 per cent of the French. The remainder have houses or bungalows. More than three-quarters of British homes have gardens, a proportion exceeded only by Luxembourg; and two-thirds have four or more rooms, second only to Luxembourg and Belgium. The

British have relatively few gadgets, but do more handyman jobs than anyone in western Europe except the Irish. More of their households (92 per cent) have television sets, and they watch them eighteen hours a week. Altogether, they spend 17 per cent of their income on housing, compared with 13 per cent for the French. All these findings, from a recent *Reader's Digest* survey, more than confirm what Price Collier noted at the beginning of the century:

> It may be a social prejudice or an ingrained habit of the British stamp of mind, but whatever it is, there can be no doubt, that the Englishman's ideal of life is to be a free man and master of the castle of his own house.

The sense of freedom in Britain, for British people, is certainly very strong. It was the British, after all, who refused to keep their identity cards once World War II was over. This was typical, I think, of something almost tangible in British life: a basic stability and certainty that may at times seem tame or innocent, but are more often upright and kindly. For centuries, Britain has escaped invasion, wars on her own soil, violent changes of government, and rule by force. Her political and administrative system was largely unaffected by the centralizing impulses of a Napoleon, a Bismarck, or a Cavour. Perhaps this is why most British people – with a few extreme exceptions – still seem confident that in the last resort the authorities are on their side. In Britain, the term "public servant" is felt to be far from meaningless: in a real sense the British still feel that policemen and other officials are there for the convenience of the citizen, and ultimately answerable to him. Although one British equivalent to the French tag, *"Il faut se défendre"*, might be "You've got to look after number one", an equally common defensive slogan is "You can't do this to me – I know my rights". Here, however aggrievedly, speaks a deep British concern for law.

Sometimes, reverence for the rules is carried to the point of parody: it gives great scope to those who enjoy stopping other people committing harmless technical offences. If the

typical hate-figure in France is a middle-aged woman concierge in a screeching argument, her equivalent in Britain
is a man in a peaked cap or apron saying with relish, "Sorry,
Sir, we're closed." Returning from France or Italy, a visitor
finds it hard to realize that the man really means it, and that
no appeals to reason or common humanity will make him
change his mind.

But this is only the obverse of Britain's comparative tran-
quillity and the relatively mild behaviour of her police. To
argue that isolated recent cases of corruption or brutality
have disproved that stereotype would be disingenuous: in this
respect Britain is still a highly civilized country, despite the
protests of some of the "new Left". That continental Europeans still think so is shown by the reasons most of them
advance for wanting Britain to join them in uniting Europe.
In the words of one resolution voted by virtually all the non-
Communist and non-Gaullist political parties and trade unions
in the Common Market's original Six, "by her traditional
respect for law and democratic institutions, Great Britain
would strengthen the very foundations of the Europe we are
building."

That sounds encouraging: but does it not ignore one final
and fundamental stereotype – British insularity? This is something attested not only by foreigners, but also by the British
themselves. Returning home in 1718 after two years' absence,
Lady Mary Wortley Montagu wrote from Dover:

I cannot help looking with partial eyes on my native land.
That partiality was certainly given us by nature, to prevent
rambling, the effect of an ambitious thirst after knowledge, which
we are not formed to enjoy. All we get by it, is a fruitless desire
of mixing the different pleasures and conveniences which are
given to different parts of the world, and cannot meet in any
one of them. After having read all that is to be found in the
languages I am mistress of, and having decayed my sight by
midnight studies, I envy the easy peace of mind of a ruddy
milk-maid, who, undisturbed by doubt, hears the sermon, with
humility, every Sunday, not having confounded the sentiments

of natural duty in her head by the vain enquiries of the schools, who may be more learned, yet, after all, must remain as ignorant. And, after having seen part of Asia and Africa, and almost made the tour of Europe, I think the honest English squire more happy, who verily believes the Greek wines less delicious than March beer; that the African fruits have not so fine a flavour as golden-pippins; that the becafiguas of Italy are not so well tasted as a rump of beef; and that, in short, there is no perfect enjoyment of this life out of Old England. I pray God I may think so for the rest of my life. . . .

"You cannot imagine what pleasure I feel," wrote Smollett in 1765,

while I survey the white cliffs of Dover. . . . Not that I am at all affected by the *nescio qua dulcedine natalis soli* of Horace.

That seems to be a kind of fanaticism, founded on the prejudices of education, which induces a Laplander to place the terrestrial paradise among the snows of Norway, and a Swiss to prefer the barren mountains of Soleure to the fruitful plains of Lombardy. I am attached to my country, because it is the land of liberty, cleanliness, and convenience; but I love it still more tenderly, as the scene of all my interesting connections, as the habitation of my friends, for whose conversation, correspondence, and esteem I wish alone to live.

Reasonable sentiments; but quite a contrast with Smollett's scornful treatment of the French. His pride in British liberty and cleanliness, like Lady Mary Wortley Montagu's love of Old England, was far surpassed by the presumption of later patriots. Price Collier, in 1901, quoted in wonderment Lord Curzon's dedication in a volume called, soberly enough, *Problems of the Far East*: "To those who believe that the British Empire is, under Providence, the greatest instrument for good that the world has ever seen. . . ." And Collier went on:

Where, in the history of mankind, may one look to find such a magnificent assumption of virtue and omniscience, coupled with incomprehensible self-satisfaction? It makes one fearful for the destinies of the race when one sees it proclaim itself thus arrogant.... Who believes that the world is better where England dominates? The English. Who believes that India is happier? The English. Who believes that Ireland is happier? The English. Who believes that the East under English protection is happier? The English. Who believes that North America is happier? The English. But what do the four hundred millions of people, controlled by these million English gentlemen, whose omniscient prophet Lord Curzon is,—what do they think? What do they say? .... This amazing assumption that England has done more for the world than any other agency, is a characteristic of these people that cannot be too often insisted upon.

Both G. J. Renier before World War II and J. H. Huizinga after it, as Dutchmen looking sympathetically at English life, were able to produce substantial "This England" anthologies of British self-satisfaction, ranging from "Our judicial system is the best in the world" to the bold *Guardian* headline "BRITISH BUN THE BEST". "We did not find an honest British bun anywhere in Europe," a gratified baker explained. Some of the sillier arguments used about the Common Market, on both sides, are of this kind. "If we had gone in at the start," argues one school, "the leadership of Europe would have been ours for the asking." "By staying out," replies another, "we shall set a moral example to the world."

But not all such feelings are quite so superficial. "The insularity of the English," wrote George Orwell,

their refusal to take foreigners seriously, is a folly that has to be paid for very heavily from time to time. But it plays its part in the English *mystique*, and the intellectuals who have tried to break it down have generally done more harm than good. At bottom it is the same quality in the English character that repels the tourist and keeps out the invader.

Like many of Orwell's remarks, this was perceptive, but not quite fair. It was geography, as much as anything, that helped keep out the invader; and geography, with history, helped to form the character that tourists found so odd.

The Roman occupation left its marks on Britain, but not all were deep: Roman law, in particular, was never fully assimilated. The Norman conquerors, as it were, went native: although William I called himself "King of the Anglo-Normans", his successors were "Kings of the English" or "of England". By the end of the fourteenth century, the Norman French spoken in Britain was so unintelligible on the continent that negotiators had to communicate in writing. The mediaeval Empire never subdued the English kingdom; and although English missionaries had helped to convert the continent and had served with Charlemagne, the mediaeval Papacy never quite subdued the English Church. The Reformation formalized that fact by schism; and for much of early modern history, England was fighting or intriguing against continental Catholic foes. Her traditional policy, not always explicit, became that of preserving the balance of power in Europe by throwing her weight into its weaker side, and always opposing attempts to unite Europe under a single rule. In terms of this habitual *Realpolitik*, her response even to Hitler was analogous to her struggle against Louis XIV, Napoleon, and Kaiser Wilhelm II.

Sitting on a coal-mine, Britain was first in the Industrial Revolution, and hence in the pressure for free trade; from this viewpoint, countries like France and Italy long seemed poor and old-fashioned, while others, like Germany later, looked like upstart rivals. Aided by the Channel to resist invasion, the British used their seamanship to found an empire early, much of it in temperate zones attractive to Europeans, and hence closely linked with the mother country. Their reaction to the 1929 crash was to extend and make systematic the beginnings of Imperial Preference. Both politically and economically, therefore, Britain stood aloof from continental Europe.

The two world wars confirmed her lofty view of it. If Belgium was the cockpit of Europe, the continent seemed to be the cockpit of the world. After World War II, it became a travel-allowance playground; but political instability seemed to be endemic there, and the separate tasks of trying to build world order through the United Nations and establishing a

Welfare State in Britain made regional unity in Europe seem both divisive and irrelevant.

In this long context, British insularity was natural; but it could hardly last. As time went on, Britain's objective status came more and more to be that of one European country among many. In military terms, this had been obvious since the later days of the war. Air-raids had already ignored the Channel; so did Hitler's primitive rockets: in the post-war world, missiles became intercontinental. Thermonuclear weapons, with their fallout, were no respecters of frontiers; nor were reconnaissance satellites: in a modern war, no country in Europe could be an island, even if surrounded by sea. Nor, even in peacetime, could Britain now afford to be insular. Like her neighbours, she needed a larger home market, a broader economic base, and greater technological resources. Without these, no European country could hold its own with the world's new giants. Painful as it might be, the best solution for Britain was to join forces with the six nations of western Europe that had formed their first "Community" in 1951, and seven years later had founded the Common Market, as the first steps to a peacefully united Europe.

This meant a change in insular habits. Intellectual arguments, as Orwell had pointed out, were hardly likely to affect them. Facts did. As Britain watched the Six struggling forward, growing more cohesive, and enjoying a steady growth that continually eluded British Chancellors, one mainstay of British insularity was gradually eroded. This was the assumption of British superiority. Many echoes of it can still be heard, often in the most altruistic places: those who over-praise Britain's record as a donor of aid to poorer countries seem often to be echoing Lord Curzon's smug pride. In both trade and aid, the record of the Six is more than comparable to Britain's; but this is widely ignored. At the same time, however, many other voices can be heard decrying the British, as if their comparative poverty and weakness in today's world were a fault of their national character, rather than a reflection of shifting balance in the international system as a whole. With so much talk in the 1950s and 1960s of "the English sickness", of "British laziness", of a supposedly unrivalled reputation for industrial strife, a new and unhappy image began to replace the more genial stereotypes recorded earlier – that of a tired, overcrowded, inward-looking island people, stuck in its ways and dazzled by past glories, incapable of facing the economic competition and diplomatic skill of its neighbours on the continent – "swinging", indeed, but frivolous and cheap. The argument, in fact, had come full circle. Opponents of British entry to the Common Market who had once maintained that Britain was too strong to need to join it now claimed that she was too weak to go in. Perhaps, after all, it was another form of insularity. "We're tops for humility" is one of the *Games People Play*. In so far as the argument fails to convince either Parliament or people, Britain's insularity may be at last on its way to the dustbin of discredited myths.

In the mirror-maze of Europe, then, some images are false; many are rough approximations; all are belied by individuals; and most are subject to change.

The same could be said of stereotypes concerning other nations: that the Spanish are lazy, hard, proud, conservative, puritanical, and passionate, as well as dyspeptic from their oily cooking; that the Belgians are mercenary gluttons, the Luxembourgers stick-in-the-muds, or the Dutch phlegmatic, stubborn, hardworking, and clean; that Switzerland is the home of punctuality, Sweden of bold voracious women, and Denmark of a sexual free-for-all. We all take legends on trust – even very ancient ones; we all see in other nations what we expect, and what we need to look for, either to bolster our self-confidence or to satisfy thwarted desires. If such folklore did not exist, it would have to be invented, if only for the tourist trade – like contemporary bars in the United States, disguised as Prohibition speakeasies, with twice-nightly raids by fake police.

But the folklore exists, and we might as well enjoy it – so

long as it leaves us free to look at shifting realities, and to see not only the genuine differences it exaggerates, but also the various features that Europeans share.

At the moment, some are more equal than others. By geography, accident, vocation, or even guile, some Europeans are already behaving like citizens of Europe while Europe is not yet built. Before finally considering what might be a European identity, it may be as well to look briefly at these equivocal pioneers.

6

Cosmopolitans

It is the customary fate of new truths to begin as
heresies and to end as superstitions.

THOMAS HENRY HUXLEY, *Science and Culture*

To see one kind of cosmopolitan, visit the Rimini riviera
on the Italian Adriatic coast. Turn away from the white
concrete hotels, the private beaches and the filling-stations,
and drive south-westwards into the afternoon sun. The road
winds and climbs; and there ahead is a mediaeval vision –
high distant ramparts, towers and battlements sharp against
the sky. Drive on, and the vision becomes solid: more hair-
pin bends, and the walls rise sheer beside the road; then a
gateway leads into the town. But this is no mere town: what
stands here on the slopes of Monte Titano is an independent
republic – San Marino, one of the smallest and oldest states
in the world.

With 23 square miles of territory, defended by a standing
army of 120 men, San Marino has been independent at least
since 885 AD. With Italy it has a customs union, and a treaty
of friendship and alliance; but until 1943 it minted its own

coinage. Its rulers are two Captains Regent chosen from among the sixty members of its elected Grand Council: despite occasional upsets, the system has lasted some 900 years. The last crisis was in 1957, when five left-wing Socialists turned Social-Democrat and overthrew the Communist majority. For a while, left-wing Councillors barricaded themselves in the Government Palace; but finally they surrendered "to avoid bloodshed", and the Italian army, which had surrounded the tiny Republic, had no cause to intervene.

San Marino sounds and looks romantic; but like Mont-St-Michel or Rocamadour, so dazzling in the distance, its reality is a shock. Inside the walls are gift shops, cafés serving fizzy sweet Moscato, and a post office frenziedly selling stamps. In a typical season, a million-and-a-half picture-postcards are sent from San Marino. Despite a few small local industries such as weaving, its 15,000 inhabitants live partly off the land and mainly off the tourists. The old and the new, the tiny republic and the polyglot mass of mainly monoglot visitors, meet uneasily behind the ramparts. The Middle Ages survive on souvenirs.

Tourists are the knights errant of Europe's new feudal society, pressing their chargers into distant lands, riding on highways instead of bridle paths, braving dragons of landladies and begging hospitality in half-completed Spanish castles, seeking the Holy Grail of a suntan or calling for White Ladies in remote inns. All told, some 50 million of them swarm through Europe every summer – a roaming population scarcely smaller than that of Britain, Germany, or France. It includes some 12 million Germans, 7 million British, 4 million Spaniards, 3½ million French, 2 million Americans, 2 million Belgians, and 1½ million Italians. In a typical year, nearly 30 million go to Italy, 20 million each to Spain and Jugoslavia, 12 million to France, 10 million to the Scandinavian countries, and 3 million to the British Isles. Flying, driving, riding in trains or coaches, cruising, hitch-hiking, bicycling, and even sometimes walking, they cover millions of miles and spend, on an average, more than 10,000 million dollars. In some cases, a country's receipts from the tourist trade make up a quarter or more of its total export earnings. In this sense, all roads in Europe lead to San Marino.

Not all this army of travellers is very cosmopolitan. Fish-and-chips in Ostend or on the Costa Brava, German beer in Belgium, French wine in Italy, or *pasta* in London, can further insulate the insular. In the Avenue de la Liberté in Luxembourg, I have actually heard one member of a dazed coach-load say to another, "No, Maud, this isn't Paris: that's where we were yesterday." Many French campers travel with portable refrigerators, television sets, and even washing machines: many British tourists – wisely – take their own tea supplies; and one prominent British opponent of entry into the Common Market is said to carry home-made British sandwiches on his rare and reluctant trips abroad. But despite these quirks, and despite the fact that travel today, as in the past, often reinforces national prejudice, the *camaraderie* of vacation clubs, camp-sites, and youth hostels is gradually fostering better knowledge of other countries, languages, and customs. The younger the travellers, the greater their sense of identity. Some of the first citizens of Europe wear headbands and flared jeans.

But these are not the only cosmopolitans. If San Marino is the type-site for tourists, the typical home of frontier-dwellers is the gabled town of Strasbourg.

Many of Europe's frontiers are curious. The Vatican City, for instance, includes the Piazza San Pietro in front of St Peter's, although there are no borders round it, and its traffic is controlled by the Italian police. The Franco-Luxembourg frontier crosses the yard of a steelworks. Further south, a Mediterranean football-ground has one goal in Monaco and the other in France. But Strasbourg stands on a far more basic dividing-line – that between the Romance and Germanic languages, which runs across Belgium, past Luxembourg, Lorraine, and Alsace, through Switzerland and across to the South Tyrol or Alto Adige: a long corridor of ambiguity and uncertainty, of confusion and sometimes conflict, that has also produced some of the founders of today's uniting Europe – Paul-Henri Spaak, Robert Schuman, and Alcide De Gasperi.

To Alsace, its frontier position brings both uneasiness and wealth. In 1931, nearly 90 per cent of its inhabitants spoke the Alsatian dialect, very similar to German; today, more than 80 per cent still do. But French, with official pressure, is making progress: 80 per cent now speak it, compared with only 55 per cent in 1931. In the local kindergarten and primary schools, the teaching of German is actually forbidden, prompting a regional magazine to define it as "a foreign language taught to children in Bordeaux and Nancy, but denied to those in Alsace for fear of grave psychological disturbances." Some Alsace patriots complain more bitterly against the inroads of Paris: "Alsace-Lorraine," declared one of them recently, "has been economically enslaved, culturally destroyed, and financially pillaged by France." And yet, at the same time, the region draws tangible benefits from its position in the heart of western Europe. Foreign firms provide more than 10 per cent of its employment, and 15,000 people cross the frontier twice a day to work in Germany and Switzerland – a striking proof that the wounds of history are healing, and that here at least the Common Market is an everyday reality.

Nor are these the only "frontier workers". Altogether, they number some 100,000, together with an uncertain and shifting population of seasonal migrants, many of them in the building trade. On a more permanent basis, just over a million citizens in the six founder-members of the Common Market work outside their own country: under the Common Market's rules, they enjoy the same pay and conditions, and the same right to seek jobs, as the nationals of the country they are in. Most of the million are unknown to the general public; but in the arts such "migrant workers" include a number of Gallicized Belgians: the novelists Georges Simenon, Françoise Mallet-Joris, and Félicien Marceau; the *cinéaste* Charles Spaak; and the popular singers Jacques Brel and Annie Cordy.

Workers from outside the Common Market – nearly 2½ million of them – have so far not been granted the benefit of non-discrimination, although representatives of both employers and trade unions are pressing for this to be done. Some find work abroad attractive, like the steelworker from Scotland who told a BBC interviewer how delighted he had been to see banks of flowers around his German factory, and to adopt the national habit of changing out of overalls into a business suit before going home. But others – Jugoslavs, Turks, Greeks, Spaniards, Austrians, Portuguese, and North Africans – are less prosperous and less well cared for. Cut off from the life of their home country, nervously sticking together, sometimes crowded into shanty-towns or virtual ghettoes, few have a chance to merge with their new background – although a few do surprisingly well for themselves. Every Sunday, the entrance hall of many European railway-stations becomes a babel of brown-skinned, bright-eyed, shabby men with foreign newspapers and sometimes cardboard suitcases, waiting for trains home or for the arrival of relatives and friends. Trying to provide for these "new Europeans" can be a frustrating and heart-breaking business. If tourists are today's international knights, some of these men look like Europe's serfdom – not so much cosmopolitans as refugees from greater poverty elsewhere.

At the opposite end of the scale is the cosmopolitanism of international capital. Its type-site used to be Monaco or Monte Carlo: today, it might be Liechtenstein, the Channel Islands, or Luxembourg.

Although independent under the Grimaldi family for many centuries, Monaco now covers only one square mile, with a population of nearly 22,000. An old Monegasque folk-song explains its plight:

> *Son Monaco, suora uno scoglio;*
> *Non semino ne raccoglio,*
> *Eppur mangiar voglio.*

> I am Monaco, high upon a rock;
> I neither sow nor reap,
> And yet I want to eat.

It won prosperity, and equivocal fame, in 1856, when Prince Charles III of Monaco authorized a gaming casino, then forbidden in France. "The name of Monaco," wrote a nineteenth-century English traveller,

has become notorious throughout Europe as the last home of the gaming-table, with the exception of the little baths of Saxony in the Valais, and the republic of Andorre, in the Pyrenees. But if you want to go to Monaco, you must take a ticket to Monte Carlo, for that is the home of Chance, who has now her pleasant abode by the sea-shore, as she had in Roman times at the Port of Antium. Monte Carlo is perhaps the culminating point of the beauty of the Riviera. The bare and precipitous rock rises high about the gazer's head. It glows with a rich and luxurious colour. Nowhere are the forms more bold and striking, or the flowers more bright and various. And yet nowhere, perhaps, are more evil passions or more dissolute characters collected together in a focus of corruption.

From then until 1914, Monaco enjoyed immense prosperity. Seventy per cent of its income came from the casino, enabling it to abolish direct taxation; and fortunes were made by those who had invested in the oddly named Sea Bathing Company, *La Société des Bains de Mer*. One of the beneficiaries was Cardinal Pecci, later to be Pope Leo XIII. But after World War I, gamblers were fewer and poorer. Soon after the 1929 crash on Wall Street and the subsequent Depression, both France and Italy raised their ban on gaming, and Monte Carlo lost further custom. By 1939, the casino's contribution to the national budget had fallen to only 30 per cent.

During and after World War II, however, the principality's fortunes changed. Under the Occupation, it became a haven for foreign capital; and after the Liberation, in spite of an agreement with France to prevent tax evasion, a number of substantial concessions were made. While Paris was thus lenient, Prince Rainier III of Monaco, in association first with

Aristotle Onassis and then with two other Balkan financiers, one of whom was later arrested, did his best to attract foreign capital. He also, in 1956, married Grace Kelly, the film-star daughter of a wealthy Philadelphia industrialist. With American help, Monaco became the legal home of large numbers of holding companies, as well as branches of such illustrious firms as Allied Chemicals, Bayer, Coca-Cola, and Johnson & Johnson.

But again the bonanza was too good to last. On Friday May 4, 1962, France lowered the boom. In a television broadcast, the Finance Minister Valéry Giscard d'Estaing denounced the "7,000 Frenchmen who are genuinely or supposedly resident" in Monaco. "I have picked out," he continued,

the names of four of them whose respective income-tax returns state their earnings as, in one case 36 million in 1960 as a broker, in another, a lady company director with an income of 35 million, and in two others sums exceeding 40 million. . . . I have looked in the Paris telephone directory, a public document. I have found their names and telephone numbers, and I have spent the evening telephoning them—only to find that three out of four of these Monaco residents were actually in Paris last night, as they no doubt frequently are. In these circumstances, one may well ask on what basis they should be exempt from income-tax.

In one instance, French tax inspectors found that a theoretically Monegasque slaughter-house was handling 10,000 head of cattle a month, but that all it had in Monaco was an office and a telephone. The general upshot was a battle that Paris easily won. Bayer, Coca-Cola, and others moved from Monaco to France; some of the holding companies transferred their headquarters to Brussels; and Prince Rainier was forced to draw in his golden horns. Monaco still survives, partly on its investments and its casino; but its place as a flourishing tax-haven has been taken by others.

Liechtenstein, a limited monarchy dating from the twelfth century, with just over sixty square miles of territory, is as rocky as Monaco but far more sombre, perched among the pine forests between Switzerland and Austria, in the Alps to the south of Lake Constance. Its total population is only 19,000, nearly a third of them foreigners; but their average income is almost the highest in Europe, second only to Sweden. Like San Marino, Liechtenstein has little agriculture, many tourists, and magnificent postage-stamps: but a fifth of its total revenue comes from the holding companies and headquarters offices attracted by its 0.1 per cent capital tax and its non-existent taxes on profits, revenue, and property. Among the companies it has sheltered have been Radio Caroline, Partex – set up to protect Svetlana Stalin's royalties, and the "Western International Ground Maintenance Organization" allegedly established by the CIA as a paymaster for Congolese mercenaries. But although Liechtenstein has a customs union with Switzerland, most of the 14,000 to 20,000 ghost firms established there seem to be German. One of the few manufacturing companies in the tiny kingdom is Ivoclar Vivadent, which produces a daily total of 75,000 false teeth, in twenty sizes and sixteen shades ranging from white to black.

Liechtenstein seems unlikely to lose these lucrative businesses; but recently other independent or semi-independent states have seen the advantages of light taxation. In the mid-1960s, some 1,500 firms established head offices in the Channel Islands – one of them quarrelling with the Swiss financial authorities over its use of the reassuring title "Swiss Jersey Bank of Commerce". More striking, if less Ruritanian, is the recent record of Luxembourg, smallest of the Common Market's founder members. Here, considerable tax concessions are offered to holding companies, especially those above a certain size; and since they are quoted on the Luxembourg stock exchange, they have access to capital throughout the Common Market. This has given the Grand Duchy an important role in the market for Eurodollars – officially defined by the Bank for International Settlements as dollars that have been acquired by a bank outside the United States and used directly or after conversion into another currency for lending to a non-bank customer, perhaps after one or more redeposits from one bank to another.

Between 1961 and 1965, total Eurodollar loans amounted to some 1,800 million dollars; in 1966 alone to 1,000 million; and in 1967, 1,756 million. When in that year the United States increased its tax on dollar exports, many American firms and groups seized on Eurodollars as a convenient substitute for their own funds, and took up 43 per cent of the Eurodollar issues – often setting up Luxembourg holding companies to manage their affairs.

In all these ways, capital has become as footloose in Europe as the tourists themselves. Some ventures, such as "offshore" investment funds operating on the American stock market from bases overseas, have recently run into trouble; but more orthodox international businesses and multinational corporations are increasingly acting as if Europe – and indeed the western world – were already united: which is one good reason for governments, trade unions, and consumers to unite in their turn in the hope of standing up to these transcontinental giants. As the giants grow, finally, they too give rise to a new kind of cosmopolitan – the international executive, part of a priesthood as powerful as the Vatican and no less rich. On current estimates, there are over 40,000 American men, women, and children living in Europe on the pay-roll of United States business, 14,000 of them in Switzerland, but many others in Paris, London, and elsewhere. Few systematic studies have been made of their habits; but in a seemingly typical family, the father works with brisk, Americanized European colleagues, the mother mixes chiefly with American wives from business, the services, and the embassies, while the children go to American or international schools. In this way many seem to live, like diplomats, in a largely free-floating environment, an expatriate deep-freeze America. One such family of my own acquaintance will take an hour's drive across a nearby frontier to buy canned or frozen fruit and vegetables at a US Army PX store, rather than go to the local market where European produce is available fresh. In the American club in Bad Godesberg, near Bonn, the illusion of being in the United States is so powerful that even the German waiters seem to have Pittsburg accents.

If international executives form a jet set, it remains relatively modest. Far less so are some of the other cosmopolitans who move across or below the surface of European life. These, the stars of the gossip columns, the sports pages, or the *Police Gazette*, are at home in several countries, as they have always been. The gossip-stars have no single type-site: their symbols are a yacht at Cannes or St-Tropez, a villa on Capri or the Côte d'Azur, an accountant or press agent in London, a lawyer or business manager in Frankfurt, and a bank account in Zurich. For a shadier *milieu*, the miniature type-site might be Andorra, that supposed paradise of smugglers; but the real habitat is more likely to be a night-club in Hamburg, a specialized *pied-à-terre* in Brussels, an arms cache in the Paris suburbs, or a secluded house in Corsica or Sicily. The outwardly respectable barons of international crime are partly figments of literary imagination; but the hard-drugs traffic, with its networks stretching from Hong Kong to Marseille, New York, Mexico, Peru, and Bolivia, is perhaps the first and certainly the deadliest common market on a world scale; while scores of otherwise banal cases confirm the increasing practice of hiring men from across a national frontier to do a single job, be paid in dollars, D-marks, or Swiss francs, then disappear again, thankful to face only Interpol, and not yet a European FBI.

The Common Market itself, moreover, has made possible new forms of large-scale fraud. In 1966, a large mill in Bavaria collected some 4 million dollars in export subsidies by selling bran to a firm in Switzerland under the guise of "high quality flour". The Swiss firm then sent it back to Germany as bran, whereupon the whole cycle started again. It was only discovered when the official statistics revealed that Germany was supposedly exporting more wheat to Switzerland than Switzerland was importing altogether. In another, similar case, an Antwerp dealer shipped a cargo of wheat back and forth between Antwerp and Rotterdam, collecting an export subsidy every time it sailed away; and a Hamburg merchant did the same with maize flour, exported under subsidy and then re-imported, duty-free, as "cattle feed". Between August 1968 and May 1969, a German firm made a further 4 million dollars in export subsidies by selling low-quality butter to Jugoslavia. On arrival, the butter was turned into "mayonnaise" by adding a spiced sauce, then re-imported at a low rate of duty. Back in Germany, a centrifuge separated off the butter, which was next re-exported to Denmark, where the same trick was repeated. In January 1971, again, Common Market officials found that butter exports to the Vatican City, with a population of only 700 people, had risen to 160 tons a year. Clearly, the subsidized butter was not being used to polish the floor of St Peter's, but to supply Italian grocers and enrich the dealers at the Common Market's expense.

Some of the sharp-eyed officials who exposed these various frauds were the often maligned "Eurocrats" of the Common Market. As international civil servants, they are not unique in Europe: the United Nations organizations in Geneva, the Bank for International Settlements in Basle, the Council of Europe in Strasbourg, and the Organization for Economic Co-operation and Development in Paris, also employ multinational staff and multilingual interpreters. But most of the Eurocrats have a distinctive *esprit de corps* and a sense of mission. The last of our cosmopolitans, in fact, share with the younger tourists some claim to be the first "citizens of Europe".

In all, 8,700 men and women staff the institutions of the European Community. 2,500 of these work in the Euratom establishments at Geel in Belgium, Ispra in Italy, Karlsruhe in Germany, and Petten in the Netherlands, engaged in peaceful nuclear research. The remaining 6,200 are officials of the Commission, the Council of Ministers, the European Parliament, the Court of Justice, and the European Investment Bank, divided between Luxembourg and Brussels; and of these the most characteristic are those employed by the Commission. It was to them, indeed, that the term "Eurocrats" was first applied, in 1961, by the then Brussels correspondent of *The Economist*, the author and journalist Margot Lyon.

My own earliest meeting with Eurocrats was in 1955, at the Luxembourg headquarters of the European Coal and Steel Community, in some ways a specialized pilot plant for the later Common Market. They then inhabited the former offices of the Luxembourg national railways, in an old rusticated brownstone building near the edge of the ravine that divides the city. Almost the first official that I saw was a burly figure climbing in through a ground-floor window to save himself a walk: it was an Englishman, François Duchêne, assistant to Jean Monnet, the President of the Community's executive High Authority; years later, he was to become the dignified head of the Institute for Strategic Studies. This informality, combined with hard work, seemed to be the keynote of the whole organization. The High Authority's Dutch Secretary-General, Edmond Wellenstein, often rode to work on an ancient-looking bicycle; and Monnet himself did much of his work in rough clothes at his house in the country. Equally typical was the presence of an English official: although the staff was fairly evenly divided between French, German, Italian, and Benelux nationals, all deliberately scrambled, from directors-general to doormen, there was also room for bright people of other nationalities. Secrets were few, and doors were open. Journalists dropped into the office on friendly terms without passes: a little later, when I myself joined the staff, the present Luxembourg Minister for Economic Affairs, then a star reporter for the "Europe" news agency, used to sit on my desk for long arguments about coal, steel, iron ore, scrap, and international politics.

In the city of Luxembourg itself, some European officials tended to play a rather colonial rôle. Unable to speak Letzeburgesch, the local patois, they smiled at Luxembourgers' accents in French or German. Often, they were irritated by the slow, claustrophobic atmosphere of what was in some respects a landlocked provincial town, with its brass-band concerts in the square on Sunday morning, its trams passing under the windows of the Grand-Ducal palace, its stout ladies in astrakhan coats eating cakes in the fashionable café, its tiny theatre, and its unresponsive shop assistants, who when asked for anything not in stock would seldom say "We have some coming in", or "You might try this", or "Perhaps So-and-so will have it", but simply, flatly, *"Non"* – adding, on occasion, "That you will never find in Luxembourg." Well paid, busy, feeling important but isolated, unafraid of local officialdom, some of these proto-Eurocrats found it hard to avoid condescending to "the natives". It was an unattractive facet of their unusual situation – the *pukka sahib* complex to which all international officials are exposed.

The best of them resisted it; and what was impressive was how many outstandingly able people had been drawn to this remote pioneering venture. Many, including most of the nine Members of the High Authority – roughly equivalent to Ministers, were World War II or Resistance veterans whose countries had recently fought each other. Some still bore bodily wounds, and others had been scarred by life in concentration camps. But the past was put behind them; and since many came from business, industry, banking, engineering, academic life, or "European" political activity, there was also little sense of being stifled by ingrained civil service routine. The few exceptions in this respect were those concerned with personnel administration – a deadly task at the best of times: the operational departments were mostly alert, informal, and imaginatively efficient.

Much of this spirit was carried over to Brussels when the Common Market Commission was set up there in 1958. This was partly because it recruited many of those who had helped to draft the Common Market treaty, and partly because it borrowed or transferred staff from the High Authority in Luxembourg. One such recruit actually appointed himself. Noting that the embryonic Commission still had no service to provide rooms, meals, and accommodation for its frequent international meetings, and having helped do just this in Luxembourg, he took the train to Brussels, walked into the half-finished Commission building, and found an empty office already supplied with a telephone. Picking it up, he ordered a desk, a chair, and stationery, then announced his name to the switchboard and the personnel department, and pinned his card on the door. For several weeks he supplied a highly efficient service, and was even paid for his trouble – until he was exposed, admonished, and offered a job.

This was characteristic of the early confusion in the Euratom and Common Market Commissions, which at first shared office buildings and even some staff. Then, gradually, the Common Market's numbers expanded into new premises and an elaborate organigram. Soon, the Belgian authorities were persuaded to allow Eurocrats special car licence plates with the letters EUR, six stars, and the appropriate numbers, all in red, white, and blue. But if this seemed to mark the newcomers as a caste apart, there was less "colonial" feeling here than in Luxembourg. Brussels is hardly Paris, but it has a vigorous and cosmopolitan life of its own, with flourishing theatres and bookshops, and a world-famous ballet company; parts of it may be ugly, but there is nothing remotely Ruritanian in its lively international atmosphere. And while Eurocrats tended to move into newly-built residential suburbs, and send their children to a polyglot European School like that they had founded in Luxembourg, there was fair scope for contacts between them and their Belgian hosts.

The Commission's first President, Walter Hallstein, was certainly more systematic and less mercurial than Jean Monnet; but his eye for talent was little less keen. In Brussels as in Luxembourg, the Eurocrats tended to be an intellectual élite, with an élite's faults and virtues; but here, as there, any potential arrogance was humbled by the interplay of six and more different nationalities, engaged together in a difficult but invigorating task. Some national stereotypes persisted. Italians seemed to be energetic but clannish, Frenchmen proudly intelligent, Germans painstaking but easily hurt, Belgians materialistic, Luxembourgers conservative, Dutchmen stubborn. But not everyone conformed to the clichés. It was even quite hard to tell one nationality from another by mere appearance: only their accents, usually, gave them away. And even those who seemed most typical of their country's traditional image, when they got together, made a lively mixture, producing sharper, better-tested ideas than any would have worked out alone.

Since those fairly early days, a number of changes have intervened. The Eurocrats' numbers have remained fairly stable. In 1971, the Commission had a total permanent staff of 5,423. Of these, 541 were translators and interpreters into the Community's four existing official languages – Dutch, French, German, and Italian, of which all Eurocrats are expected to manage at least two. Three hundred of them were porters, doormen, messengers, drivers, and so on; 2,025 were secretaries and typists; 1,040 were administrative assistants; and only 1,517 were fully-fledged officials. Large as these numbers may seem, they remain small compared with national civil services. The Commission's work is obviously not meant to replace or duplicate that of its national counterparts; but its responsibilities range over a vast area and many different subjects, including trade, aid, finance, labour policy, transport, agriculture, research and technology, atomic and other energy, regional policy, coal and steel, health, statistics, and foreign relations. Given so much to cope with, the Eurocrats can hardly be accused of obeying Parkinson's Law. At the same time, however, their morale has suffered from a number of other ills.

One is the mere fact that the Common Market is now thirteen years old. All institutions risk growing tired; and with the completion of the Community's tariff-cutting process in 1968 the easiest part of its work was over. It now faced, and faces, the dull, mammoth task of gradually building a full economic and monetary union, involving not only political difficulties, but also countless detailed arguments about a host of subjects, each of which in isolation tends to look petty and bureaucratic.

If this were not enough, morale has also been affected by the ceaseless verbal and protocol sniping of General de Gaulle, punctuated by Jupiter-like interventions intended to cut the

Commission down to size. It was one thing to be insulted by the General's gibes about "stateless technocrats": it was quite another to face the 1963 veto on Britain's first attempt to join the Common Market, and the constitutional crisis two years later, when France virtually withdrew from the Community institutions for a full seven months. Independent surveys conducted among the Eurocrats at the time confirmed their gloom and anger. While some still optimistically saw the General as a "European" *malgré lui*, the vast majority held that he had gravely damaged European unity, and even more would have voted against him as a "first President for Europe". The damage, and the bitterness, were to last a long time.

One final but not negligible fact helped sap morale in the late 1960s. This was the Commission's move into a huge new building – "a fatal sign," said one political scientist. The building in question, the Berlaymont, is a grandiose, X-shaped, 14-storey structure of steel, glass, and concrete, looking a little like some strange spare part for a giant's automobile. Inside, it has broad carpeted lobbies on each landing, and curved identical corridors flanked by numbered doors receding into what seems an endless distance. The impression is that of a great empty liner, possibly from *Outward Bound*. Without a map or compass, the visitor has trouble working out which leg or arm of the X he happens to be in, and which corridor of that. Nor are visitors the only sufferers. The staff bulletin overflows with complaints about the building. Only the windows on the top floors can be opened; in hot weather, those facing south are roasted; in cold, the central heating grills some and leaves others freezing; and the ventilation system of the underground garages sends narcotic fumes into workrooms and conference halls, putting audiences to sleep even more effectively than some of their speakers. The whole place is a setting for a Jacques Tati satire – soulless, alien, dwarfing, and not even efficient or cheap.

And yet, the Eurocrats survive; and so does much of their spirit. Since the departure of General de Gaulle and the Hague "summit" meeting of the original Common Market Six in

December 1969, at which it was agreed to strengthen and enlarge the Community, the practical idealism of Brussels has once more revived. The new Commission which took office in July 1970 included several much younger men than its predecessors, as well as the veteran federalist militant Altiero Spinelli; and eighteen months later, when the British negotiations for membership were at last successful, the new prospect for the Eurocrats seemed bright.

Are they, as two American observers have suggested, "the vanguard of Europa"? In a simplistic sense, certainly not. When the Coal and Steel Community's institutions were established, the "model" at the back of its founders' minds was undoubtedly that of a "Government of Europe". World War II was only lately over; Allied military government was still a familiar concept; and the very name of the "High Authority", independent of governments and conceivably their superior, recalled that of the International Ruhr Authority, wielding power from above. "Supranationalism" was then a favourite slogan. In practice, the High Authority proved far less autocratic than its name or even its theoretical powers: it kept its independence and its Community-wide responsibility, but it acted in concert – in "dialogue", to use Community jargon – with the Council of Ministers whose members were national representatives, much as the Common Market Commission was later to do. In the Common Market itself, this "dialogue" became more complex, with filter and feedback through innumerable committees. No existing national constitution provides a precedent for this delicate but tough interplay of legal power, expertise, political pressure, enlightened self-interest, recommendations, veiled threats, bait, equity, and the recognition of economic necessity that constitutes the Community system. To suppose, therefore, that the Commission will one day simply evolve into a Cabinet, the European Parliament into a House of Representatives, and the Council of Ministers into a Senate, while Europe's nations turn into the equivalent of American States, would be absurdly optimistic or gloomy, according to taste.

Nevertheless, the Community system is far more closely-knit, and far more capable of further growth, than that of a traditional international organization, with a merely administrative secretariat answerable to a council of national ministers. The Commission remains independent of the Ministers: it has the right of initiative, and the power to take Governments to Court; within carefully prescribed limits, it has executive powers. The Council decides on all fundamental matters; but it has not completely relinquished majority voting, and it has conceded minor powers to the Parliament, and some fiscal autonomy to the Commission. The Parliament is not yet directly elected; but fresh moves are afoot in this direction, and the pressure for greater power will grow as a result of British membership. The Court of Justice, finally, has very considerable legal power, and a growing body of European jurisprudence. What is more, the process of economic integration itself has a certain autonomy. The removal of tariff barriers exposes other hindrances and distortions of trade, and raises demands that they be abolished. The need for fair competitition involves joint action in economic policy. The difficulty of competing with other economic giants is an incentive to join forces in larger units. The dangers and uncertainties of the international monetary system are a spur to joint action in Europe, as much as in the West as a whole. Drawn by necessity, prodded by the Community's institutions, its member states seem certain to go on lurching towards unity; and in this respect the Eurocrats may well be "the harbingers of Europa" – although few would care to define its political structure in advance.

Seen from Brussels, in fact, Europe's future looks both pragmatic and complex: simplistic models seem out of place. The fear of losing national sovereignty looks less real than the danger of clinging to its shadow and losing the chance of genuine collective influence – delaying too long the joint European action in monetary matters, defence, and foreign policy that today's and tomorrow's problems demand.

But to act wholeheartedly together, more is needed than

mere cosmopolitanism. Even international élites – even half-suffocated Eurocrats – are powerless against national inertia. And to mobilize Europe's potential energies, its nations will have to acquire something of the *esprit de corps* that Eurocrats and others feel – recognizing, valuing, and using national differences, but acknowledging also some sense of identity as Europeans, in a way that still seems unnatural to many who have not yet shared Community experience. At the end of the day, is such a thing possible? What real identity, finally, does western Europe have?

7

A European Identity

Nature has made it difficult for the different parts of
Europe to live in peace. But it has also made it impossible for them to live in isolation.

R. H. TAWNEY, *Why Britain Fights*

DESPITE appearances and folklore, Europeans have much
in common. Their problem is to realize the fact, and act
upon it, without having to invoke nostalgic sentimentality or
the bogy of some common enemy.

Geologically, their continent is a unit, including its islands,
but one that merges imperceptibly into the Asian East. Even
the Urals are no longer a barrier; and *Mitteleuropa* is as much
a matter of terrain as of human society. Many of the continent's political troubles stem from this simple geographical
fact: *les incertitudes allemandes* are mirrored by the "defensive expansionism" of Russia; and as a Germanic Arthur Hugh
Clough might have written, "Eastward, look, the land is
breit." Fear of the East, and repeated invasions from it, have
left deep furrows in the West's collective unconscious; one of
the tasks for a European political Community will undoubtedly be to exorcise some of that legacy by establishing

either firmer frontiers or, more hopefully, a *modus vivendi* that lessens suspicions on both sides. One psychological clue that might prove helpful is mutual fascination. The post-war restoration of Danzig could hardly have been more meticulous if the Germans had done it themselves; and no one can talk long or deeply with a thoughtful German without realizing that the *Ostpolitik*, whatever its limits, is a necessary state of mind. No nation can live for ever with its back to the Berlin wall.

Open to the East, the continent of Europe has long been aimed, as it were, at the West, and even at Britain. Europe's mountain ridges run roughly east and west, making for ease of lateral movement: in western Europe, the psychological opposites are north and south, Nordic and Latin; in prehistoric and even classical times, Britain was part of the northern region – no maritime power, but firmly linked to the mainland, first by a land bridge, then by easily crossed straits. Only later did history accentuate her isolation and help to foster an insular frame of mind.

A promontory of Asia, tamed by the sea and made fertile by the weather, western Europe's varied nooks and crannies made a fruitful home from home for those who invaded her. Their ultimate origins, even their separate strains, seem unimportant beside the plain fact that the so-called "races of Europe" form a single interrelated dynasty, a vast people of intermarried cousins, with only a few hermit nations living bear-like in the mountains, virtually untouched by human hand. Cousins can quarrel, and these did: but battle-slogans, even in Gothic print with learned footnotes, need not be taken as eternal truth.

The same applies to Europe's languages. "Beef" and "cow", so often quoted in textbooks on Norman England to contrast the conquerors' French with their vassals' English, both ultimately derive from the Indo-European "*gwous*". Perhaps one day American and English will become as mutually incomprehensible; but this need not wind up the English-Speaking Union: it would merely have to change its name. And if fewer people worried about linguistic "purity", life might even grow much easier: already, a kind of English seems to be seeping over Europe in the wake of the tourist crusades.

Go far enough back, then, and identity seems almost within reach. But who, today, could identify with the Beaker Folk, still less with Cro-Magnon man? The real barriers are closer to us; and yet even they have less substance than we think. Blinded by proximity and our concern for detail, we tend to miss the largest lettering on the map of history – that which spans the mountains and even the North Sea.

Greece and Rome: a signpost phrase that points to dubious generalizations; but no western-European language or mental vocabulary is free of their legacy. *"Polis"*, "politics", "policy", "polite"; "democracy"; "justice" – the classical influence is more than a matter of linguistics. We know very well that Greek democracy was undemocratic, and Roman justice unjust: but we also know that the strands of meaning entwined in the modern words, and in the thoughts and emotions that go with them, are common to all our countries, in a sense that in parts of Asia they are not. Latin, in particular, has left us a political heritage, not only in Roman law, more deeply impressed on the mainland than on Britain, but also in Roman values, the words for which, at least, were as readily accepted in the British Isles as elsewhere. Authority, constancy, discipline, faith, gravity, humanity, liberty, and piety sound old-fashioned, as indeed they are. Different nations, like different age-groups, may rank them in different orders of preference: but we all believe we understand them, and each other. We also understand, if only from political speeches, the essential notion of a universal community – another common legacy from Rome.

Many Catholic advocates of a united Europe place great stress upon the Middle Ages as its earliest embodiment; but this seems both unattractive and untrue. Admittedly, both Pope and Emperor asserted universal pretensions; but closer examination suggests that most of their time was spent in the struggle to give their claims some substance. Blow for blow, the ages of imperial unity were as strife-ridden as those of modern nationalism, until the present century; and those of Papal faith were much the same. The records, moreover, flatter the concepts they embodied: most Europeans' perception of what was "really" happening was probably local, but has failed to survive because they had little reason to write it down. Even Charlemagne's empire, so strikingly coincident with the borders of the original Common Market Six, was short-lived and rather artificial: the "Carolingian Renaissance" was a gathering of talent rather than a spontaneous outburst. As for the Crusades, they undoubtedly helped to reinforce Europe's sense of self-righteous and beleaguered unity; but at the cost of highly unChristian behaviour and great unpopularity among those who had to foot the bill.

The true significance of the Middle Ages, as contributing to a possible sense of European identity, was precisely the illusion that they fostered. The rise of nation-states, and the divisions of the Reformation, gave previous ages a retrospective glamour: then, it was felt, before the deluge, in the golden dawn, there had been a unity in Christendom – roughly conterminous with Europe – that fallen modern man had lost. It was not the first time, nor the last, that history was used as a screen on which to project some cherished fantasies; but the interest of it, in this context, was the encouragement it gave to political theorists seeking "models" for the better ordering of international affairs.

This, in a sense, was the true motive of the various proposals for "European unity" that began to be made from the fourteenth century onwards. Essentially, they were universal in scope. Europe, in a word, was the universe: there was no point or hope in seeking unity with barbarians. Pierre Dubois, Antoine Marigny, the Duc de Sully, Leibniz, Emeric Crucé, William Penn, and the Abbé de Saint Pierre – all in their time produced plans for European or Christian Councils, Diets, Assemblies, and even Armies, some of them in the hope of ensuring perpetual peace. At the time, their quest was about as fruitful as the twentieth-century efforts of world federalists, and its motives were very similar: but they left some trace in European thinking – as, it may be hoped, world federalists may also do. They formed, as it were, a priming or undercoat for later, more successful ventures, and need not be scorned because their work is now lost to view.

The cosmopolitanism of the eighteenth century, like that of today's Europe, may also have contributed to the priming process. The founding of the United States of America certainly did. George Washington himself foresaw a "United States of Europe", well in advance of Victor Hugo, one of whose speeches on the subject was greeted with cries of "These poets!" and "Hugo's gone mad!" The notion reappeared, most notably, in a memorandum prepared in 1930 by Aristide Briand; but it was not until after World War II that a layer of reality was given to all these idealistic plans.

Such, very briefly, is the common background that makes a European identity possible to conceive. But conception is not realization; and the divided history of modern Europe, as we have seen, gave rise to far stronger rival conceptions on a national scale. Wars within Europe were seen not as general, shared calamities, but as national struggles to defend one's country or enlarge its borders, to right or to upset the famous "balance of power". Yet it takes only a mental somersault to transpose Europe's eighteenth-century wars to a modern African or mediaeval Byzantine context, in order to see them as a collective malady rather than the clash of two or more noble, disinterested, virtuous, heroic, and thoroughly likeable antagonists, each of whom appeared to the other the blackest of traitors, villains, egotists, and cowards.

The necessary somersault came in the later years of World War I. To anyone looking back now, under the age of fifty, the emotions of 1914 seem incomprehensible. Men marching off to death in the trenches, eagerly, as a patriotic duty; songs proclaiming "We don't want to lose you, but we know you've got to go"; belief in lying atrocity stories and tales of Russians with snow on their boots – the whole frenzied fabric seems like solemn lunacy. Why on earth was anyone fighting?

What principle was involved? What interest was at stake to warrant such a massacre? Our fathers and grandfathers were sure of the answer: but certainty began to falter as the years dragged on. "Disillusion", and pacifist literature, were the post-war result: "pure" patriotism, of the jingoistic, "my country, right or wrong" variety became rarer as an explicit belief.

World War II seems at first sight a somersault backwards. The generation that remembers it might appear as deluded as that of 1914. Already, some historians have suggested – implausibly – that Adolf Hitler was a "normal" statesman pushed to excess by the democracies. Was World War II just a further instalment in power politics, dressed up as an ideological crusade against Nazism because "pure" patriotism no longer appealed? The short, definitive answer is No. The war against Hitler was a war against racism and the death camps, tyranny, brutality, and triumphant ignorance: it had to be fought. But fighting it, whatever the overspill from patriotic songs and slogans, failed to reinstate – thank goodness – the chauvinist lunacy of a generation earlier. This time, there was little talk of "squeezing Germany till the pips squeaked"; and the Morgenthau Plan, which would have "pastoralized" the defeated enemy, was dropped even sooner than the kindred ban on "fraternization" between the Germans and the post-war occupation forces. Whatever the mistakes and follies of the years after World War II, the mental somersault of World War I had been permanent, and Winston Churchill's motto, "In Victory: Magnanimity", was allowed to prevail.

Thus it was that the slaughter of the World War I trenches had its delayed effect: World War II was a scavenging operation only. The phrase so often applied to it – "Europe's last civil war" – is better left for World War I, since that was the last convulsion of the *ancien régime*. At last it had become obvious that all European countries must make peace with each other, or perish.

This brought them closer to an identity of interests: but a

true European identity was still far off. In the post-war period, however, it drew closer, partly because it began to be possible to define Europe's identity by contrast with opposites.

Such definition by opposites was a familiar proceeding: classical geographers had used it to distinguish Europe from Asia and Africa; mediaeval man had contrasted Christians with barbarians; modern travellers and travel-writers had praised Europe's wealth and sophistication at the expense of the rest of the globe. Now, however, the contrasts available were clearer and closer.

One was with Eastern Europe. Not on any human or cultural basis, nor even with a sense of hostility: there was and is much sympathy with Poles, Czechs, and other victims of Soviet power. But the extension of Communist rule in Eastern Europe, and the brutal means that were often used to achieve it, made western democracy, for all its faults, look very much more attractive. As it is, all the present and impending members of the European Common Market enjoy a degree of free speech and political choice denied to most of their eastern neighbours. Not all have effectively multi-party democracies – but this is not on account of governmental repression. If the French and Italian Left were to regroup themselves into viable alternative Governments, the virtual monopolies at present enjoyed by the majority parties would come to an end. It may be argued that this is impossible "under the capitalist system"; but still more cogent is the opposite argument – that what prevents it is the nature of the Communist parties in both Italy and France. Here, then, is one immediate element in western Europe's identity: democracy, warts and all. By itself, of course, the contrast with eastern Europe is no necessary argument for unity in the West. The days of "rollback" theory, when the doves of peace spoke warlike metaphors, and a united Europe was seen as a bastion against "Soviet aggression" and a force of attraction to peel the "satellite" countries away from Russia, are fortunately at an end. But if one hopes to join forces with one's neighbours, there can be comfort in the assurance that they are far from being police states.

The second contrast is with America. This, too, should not be taken as an unfriendly gesture. As far as the political instruments of democracy go, the United States resembles most of western Europe. But it differs in many obvious ways. One, made much of by those who put the economic case for European unity, is American wealth: by most material standards, Americans are about twice as rich as Europeans; and to attain a similar level, there can be little doubt that Europe needs to unite. But equally important, once wealth is achieved, is the use that society makes of it; and here significant differences of priority seem to emerge. The United States spends rather less than 10 per cent of its gross domestic product on social security: all the present and impending members of the Common Market spend between 11 and 16 per cent – something approaching twice as much. This is a startling contrast; and it seems to reflect a contrast in social philosophy. A fact of American history that can easily be overlooked is the fierce struggle for industrial wealth that took place in the nineteenth century. With astonishing rapidity, matched only by current efforts in China, the country was wrenched from an agrarian to an industrial way of life in a few short generations. The scars of that surgery are still obvious in the raw ugliness and hints of brutality of which even the friendliest European visitors sometimes complain. Similar sights can be seen, of course, in Europe; but they are less extensive, and are better hidden by the patina of history and century-long grooming that much of Europe's landscape enjoys. Now, with typically intent thoroughness, Americans are beginning their own grooming process – just as some European cities seem to be starting in the opposite direction. But if Europe does succeed in matching American prosperity, or in lagging less dramatically behind it, many Europeans hope that they will be able to profit from what they regard as America's mistakes. Should they fail to unite, they fear that their comparative poverty may expose them to the inroads of American business. Needing all the capital they could find, they would be less able to impose restraints on its exploitation – anti-pollution laws, regional planning, and so on. As one French Eurocrat characteristically put it, "What we want is to produce food as tasty as ours on an American industrial scale." For "food" read "a way of life and prosperity", and this seems a respectable ideal.

The third and final contrast that helps to define Europe's identity is the contrast with the world's poor. Against this, the contrasts with eastern Europe and the United States shrink drastically: all these northern countries are plutocrats by comparison with the southern hemisphere. The distortions in the mirror-maze of national stereotypes are as nothing beside swollen bellies and limbs like sticks. Should Europeans, then, turn aside from the "inward-looking" task of uniting in order to concentrate on aid programmes? To suppose so is to fall into the ancient economic trap of believing that redistribution is a substitute for creating wealth. Both are necessary; and Europe will be in a better position, economically and politically, to help where help is needed, if her separate nations join forces. What hinders liberal import policies? The need to protect high-cost industries at home. What keeps the high-cost industries in being? A slowly growing economy incapable of offering new jobs for those at present badly employed. What would assist growth? A larger market and common policies for expansion. What would achieve that? Unity in Europe, as a step towards freer trade and more stable markets in the world.

The argument by contrast is essentially an argument from the present, just as the argument of a common heritage is clearly an argument from the past. But since the quest for a European identity is finally a search for a European future, what sort of future Europe can we reasonably seek?

First, and most obviously, a peaceful Europe. War between western European countries now seems a remote possibility; but so long as the German people remain divided, and strains occur within the eastern system, conflict with the East is a potential danger. For this reason, a European political Community will be obliged to pursue a continuing dialogue with its eastern neighbours, either separately or collectively: and its own cohesion will remove one source of possible conflict, in Germany itself.

Secondly, with the United States, Europe would seek to assert a distinct but not totally separate identity. Too many ties rightly link the two continents for either to become the "third force" once beloved of Gaullist philosophers. Europe, with its small, highly populated area, is far too vulnerable to seek to develop its own independent nuclear defence. But it might with advantage combine its conventional forces, and speak with a single voice in the monetary and military spheres, as it already does in the fields of economics and trade.

Thirdly, in its relations with the world's poorer countries, Europe's identity would be affirmed by the extension to them of the same concern for social welfare that it has painfully and slowly learned to exercise at home. Disraeli's "two nations" are now two hemispheres; and tragic and dangerous consequences could flow from a failure to see the world as Europe's great nineteenth-century reformers saw their own society.

To the East, in other words, Europe must show its firm and confident patience; to the West, its common sense and moderation; and to the South, its intelligent compassion.

Do Europeans really share these qualities? Is this not an unrealistic picture of a group of grasping foreigners, unlike ourselves of course? The question might be put by any nation in Europe, in any language. Can we (you, they) trust them (us, you)?

I can only give a personal answer. My own experience of working in and with the Common Market, for its leaders and founders, alongside colleagues of various nationalities, and in all its member countries, leads me to the firm belief that despite all national clichés – some of them true – our European neighbours are as various and yet as homogeneous as ourselves. No nation has a monopoly of saints or criminals; the differences within any one people are far greater than the average difference between peoples. Seek out your like, and you will find it anywhere in Europe: look for an enemy, and that too will be an easy quest. What differentiates us, in fact, is less our supposed "national character" than the social and economic context that works so deeply on our original clay; and since in the present world all European countries have shrunk to a modest size in a modest continent, we are all much more alike than we think. Fortunately, however, the mirror-maze remains open. No power on earth can stop us being ourselves.

For Further Reference

1 In Search of a Tribe

Burke, Edmund. *Letters on a Regicide Peace*. London, 1796.

Delamater, John; Katz, Daniel; & Kelman, Herbert C. "On the nature of national involvement: a preliminary study", *Journal of Conflict Resolution*, Vol. XIII, No. 3 (September, 1969), pp. 320-57.

Frémy, D. & M. (edd.) *Quid?* Paris, 1971.

Gilbert, W. S. *Iolanthe*. London, 1882.

James, Henry. *The Europeans*. New York, 1878.

Katz, Daniel; Kelman, Herbert C.; & Vassiliou, Vasso. "A Comparative approach to the study of nationalism", *Papers of the Peace Research Society*, No. 14. Ann Arbor, Michigan, 1969.

Mayne, Richard. *The Community of Europe*. London, 1962; New York, 1963.

Voltaire, François Marie Arouet de. *Poème de Fontenoy*, in *Oeuvres complètes*, Paris, 1785-9.

Voyenne, Bernard. *Histoire de l'idée Européenne*. Paris, 1964.

2 A Promontory of Asia

Caesar, Julius. *The Conquest of Gaul*. Transl. S. A. Handford. London, 1951.

Chabod, Federico. *Storia dell'Idea d'Europa*. Paperback edition, Bari, 1967.

Donne, John. *Complete Poetry and Selected Prose*. London, 1929.

Dury, G. H. *The Face of the Earth*. London, 1959.

Gottmann, Jean. *A Geography of Europe*. 2nd ed., London, 1954.

Heaton, Herbert. *Economic History of Europe*. New York, 1936.

Hoffman, George W. (ed.). *A Geography of Europe*. London, 1953.

Hopp, Zinken. *Norwegian Folklore*. Bergen, 1959.

Hoskins, W. G. *The Making of the English Landscape*. London, 1955.

Laborde, E. D. *Western Europe*. London, 1962.

Lawrence, D. H. *Sea and Sardinia*. London, 1923.

Mayne, Richard. "France 1969", *The Listener*, June 26, 1969.

Rousseau, Jean-Jacques. *Extrait du projet de paix perpétuelle de M. l'Abbé de Saint-Pierre*, in *Oeuvres complètes*, Paris, 1782.

Shackleton, Margaret Reid. *Europe: A Regional Geography*. London, 1939.

Stamp, L. Dudley. *Britain's Structure and Scenery*. London, 1946.

Stamp, L. Dudley. *Europe and the Mediterranean*. New edition, London, 1961.

Strabo. *Geographica*. Oxford, 1893.

3 The Melting-Pot

Alsop, Joseph. *From the Silent Earth*. London, 1965.

Carlyle, Thomas. *Sartor Resartus*. London, 1838.

Childe, V. Gordon. *The Dawn of European Civilization*. IVth ed., London, 1947.

Clark, Graham & Piggott, Stuart. *Prehistoric Societies*. New ed., London, 1970.

Daniel, Glyn. *The First Civilizations*. London, 1968.

Daniel, Glyn. *The Megalith Builders of Western Europe*. London, 1963.

Daniel, Glyn. *The Origins and Growth of Archaeology*. London, 1967.

Edwards, I. E. S. *The Pyramids of Egypt*. New ed., London, 1961.

Fleure, H. J. & Davies, M. *A Natural History of Man in Britain*. New ed., London, 1971.

Geipel, John. *The Europeans*. London, 1969.

Houston, J. M. *A Social Geography of Europe*. London, 1963.

Hutchinson, R. W. *Prehistoric Crete*. London, 1968.

Laming, Annette. *Lascaux*. London, 1959.

Landström, Björn. *Sailing Ships*. London, 1969.

Lantier, Raymond. *La vie préhistorique*. Paris, 1965.

Paor, Liam de. *Archaeology: An Illustrated Introduction*. London, 1967.

Renfrew, Colin. "Revolution in Prehistory", *The Listener*, December 31, 1970 & January 7, 1971.

Stacul, Giorgio. *Arte della Sardegna Nuragica*. Milan, 1961.

Stern, Philip van Doren. *Prehistoric Europe*. London, 1969.

Thom, Alexander. "The Megaliths of Carnac", *The Listener*, December 31, 1970.

4 Warring Tongues

Alcock, Antony. *The History of the South Tyrol Question*. London, 1970.

Barber, C. L. *The Story of Language*. London, 1964.

Barnett, Lincoln. *History of the English Language*. New ed., London, 1970.

Benveniste, Emile. *Le Vocabulaire des institutions indo-européennes*. Paris, 1969.

Boswell, James. *Journal of a Tour to the Hebrides*. London, 1786.

Bradley, Henry. *The Making of English*. New ed., London, 1968.

Chadwick, H. M. *The Nationalities of Europe*. Cambridge, 1945.

Etiemble, René. *Parlez-vous franglais?* Paris, 1964.

Ewert, Alfred. *The French Language*. London, 1933.

Foster, Brian. *The Changing English Language*. London, 1968.

Guiraud, Paul. *Les Mots étrangers*. Paris, 1965.

Héraud, Guy. *Peuples et langues d'Europe*. Paris/Milan, 1966.

Herder, Johann Gottfried von. *Uber den Ürsprung der Sprache*. Weimar, 1772.

Keyserling, Hermann Alexander. *Das Spektrum Europas*. Darmstadt, 1928.

Kraus, Karl. *Die Sprache*. New ed., Munich, 1969.

Lyon, Margot. *Belgium*. London, 1971.

Madariaga, Salvador de. *Englishmen, Frenchmen, Spaniards*. London, 1928.

Madariaga, Salvador de. *Portrait of Europe*. London, 1952; new ed., London, 1967.

Mayne, Richard. "Parlez-vous Desperanto?", *Encounter*, Vol. XXIII, No. 1, July, 1964.

Mounin, Georges. *Histoire de la linguistique*. Paris, 1967.

Parkes, Mercedes Gallagher. *Introduction to Keyserling*. London, 1934.

Siegfried, André. *L'Ame des peuples*. Paris, 1950.

Vendryes, Joseph. *Le Langage*. Paris, 1923.

Wilson, R. A. *The Miraculous Birth of Language*. London, 1937.

5 Rogues' Gallery

Action Committee for the United States of Europe. *Statements and Declarations 1955-67*. London, 1969.

Allport, G. W. *The Nature of Prejudice*. New York, 1954.

Ardagh, John. *The New French Revolution*. London, 1968.

Arnold, Matthew. *Discourses in America*. London, 1885.

Arnold, Matthew. *Essays in Criticism*. London, 1865.

Ascham, Roger. *The Scholemaster*. London, 1570.

Avril, Pierre. *Politics in France*. Transl. John Ross, London, 1969.

Barrès, Maurice. *Au service de l'Allemagne*. Paris, 1905.

Barzini, Luigi. *The Italians*. London, 1964.

Belloc, Hilaire. *The Path to Rome*. London, 1902.

Bennett, Arnold. *Paris Nights*. London, 1913.

Bennett, Arnold. *Things That Have Interested Me*. London, 1922.

Béraud, Henri. *Gringoire, passim*. Paris, 1935.

Bismarck, Otto von. *Table Talk During the French Campaign*. Berlin, 1870-1.

Bossuet, Jacques Bénigne. *Oraisons*. Paris, 1669-87.

Boswell, James. *Boswell on the Grand Tour: Italy, Corsica, and France*. Ed. Frank Brady & Frederick A. Pottle, London, 1955.

Boswell, James. *The Life of Samuel Johnson, LL.D.* London, 1791.

Boutmy, E. *Essai d'une psychologie politique du peuple anglais au XIXe siècle*. Paris, 1901.

Brinton, Crane. *The Americans and the French*. Cambridge, Mass., 1967.

Brogan, D. W. *French Personalities and Problems*. London, 1946.

Browning, Oscar, *et al. Picturesque Europe*. London, n.d.

Brunacci, G. *Il Libro della Geografia*. Milan, 1966.

Buchanan, William & Cantrill, Hadley. *How Nations See Each Other*. Urbana, Ill., 1953.

Butor, Michel. *La Modification*. Paris, 1957.

Calleo, David. *Britain's Future*. London, 1968.

Campbell, Harriet. *A Journey to Florence in 1817*. London, 1951.

Campe, J. H. *Reise durch England und Frankreich*. Brunswick, 1803.

Campos, Christophe. *The View of France*. Oxford, 1965.

Čapek, Karel. *Letters from England*. Transl. Paul Silver. London, 1925.

Carlyle, Margaret. *Modern Italy*. London, 1957.

References

Chastenet, Jacques. *L'Angleterre d'aujourd'hui*. Paris, 1965.

Cipolla, Carlo M. *European Culture and Overseas Expansion*. London, 1970.

Claudel, Paul. *Journal*. Paris, 1960.

Clough, A. H. *Amours de Voyage*. Xth ed., London, 1883.

Cohen-Portheim, Paul. *England, the Unknown Isle*. Transl. Alan Harris, London, 1930.

Cohen-Portheim, Paul. *The Spirit of France*. Transl. Alan Harris, London, 1933.

Collier, Price. *England and the English from an American Point of View*. New York, 1909.

Commynes, Philippe de. *Cronique et Histoire du roy Louis onziesme*. Paris, 1524.

Craik, Mrs. *Fair France*. London, 1871.

Custine, Astolphe de. *Mémoires et voyages*. Paris, 1830.

Daninos, Pierre. *Les Carnets du Major Thompson*. Paris, 1952.

Defaucompret, J. B. *Londres et ses habitants*. Paris, 1817.

de Gaulle, Charles. *Vers l'Armée de métier*. Paris, 1934.

Demolder, E. *L'Agonie d'Albion*. Paris, 1901.

de Staël, Germaine. *De l'Allemagne*. New ed., Paris, 1968.

d'Harcourt, Robert. *Les Allemands et nous*. Paris, 1945.

Dickens, Charles. *Pictures from Italy*. London, 1888.

Distelbarth, P. *Lebendiges Frankreich*. Frankfurt, 1936.

Douglas, Norman. *Alone*. New ed., London, 1940.

Duby, Georges & Mandrou, Robert. *A History of French Civilization*. Transl. J. B. Atkinson, London, 1966.

Dumas, Alexandre. *Swiss Travel*. Ed. C. H. Parry, London, 1890.

Dürer, Albrecht. *Letter from Venice to Pirkheimer*, February 7, 1506.

Eckermann, Johann Peter. *Gespräche mit Goethe*. Weimar, 1836-8.

Eich, Hermann. *The Unloved Germans*. Transl. Michael Glenny, London, 1965.

Ellis, Havelock. *The Genius of Europe*. London, 1950.

Emerson, R. W. *English Traits*. Boston, 1856.

Ervine, St John. *God's Soldier*. London, 1934.

European Communities, Commission. *Basic Statistics*. Brussels/Luxembourg, annual.

European Community, February 1970.

European Economic Community, Commission. *Report on the Economic Situation in the Countries of the Community*. Brussels/Luxembourg, 1958.

187

The Europeans

Anny Fay. *Music-study in Germany*. London, 1881.
Fielding, Henry. *Journal of a Voyage to Lisbon*. London, 1755.
Forman, H. J. *Grecian Italy*. London, 1927.
Frémy, D. & M. *Quid?* Paris, 1971.
Froissart, Jean. *Chroniques*. Paris, c. 1495.
Gibbs, Philip. *European Journey*. London, 1934.
Goethe, Johann Wolfgang. *Italian Journey*. Transl. W. H. Auden & Elizabeth Mayer, London, 1962.
Goldsmith, Oliver, *The Citizen of the World*. London, 1762.
Grand-Carteret, J. *La Femme en Allemagne*. Paris, 1887.
Grenadou, Ephraïm & Prevost, Alain. *Grenadou: paysan français*. Paris, 1966.
Grindrod, Muriel. *Italy*. New ed., London, 1966.
Grube, G. W. *Geographische Charakterbilder*. Berlin, 1878.
Hale, J. R. *England and the Italian Renaissance*. New ed., London, 1963.
Haller, Theodor. *This Way Please, eine heitere Anleitung zum richtigen Gebrauch der Engländer*. Basel, 1952.
Halsey, Margaret. *With Malice Towards Some*. London, 1938.
Hamerton, P. G. *The Intellectual Life*. London, 1873.
Harms, H. *Landerkunde von Europa*. Berlin, 1911.
Hegel, G. W. F. *Werke*. Heidelberg, 1832-45.
Heine, Heinrich. *Italian Travel Sketches*. Transl. Elizabeth A. Sharp, London, n.d.
Heppenstall, Rayner. *The Fourfold Tradition*. London, 1961.
Hoffman, Stanley et al. *In Search of France*. Cambridge, Mass., 1963.
Holmes, Oliver Wendell. *Our Hundred Days in Europe*. London, 1893.
Huddleston, Sisley. *France and the French*. New ed., London, 1928.
Huizinga, J. H. *Confessions of a European in England*. London, 1958.
Huizinga, J. H. *Postmerk Londen*. Amsterdam, 1945.
Hyatt, Alfred H. (ed.) *The Charm of Venice*. London, 1908.
James, Henry. *A Little Tour in France*. Boston, 1885.
James, Henry. *Parisian Sketches*. New York, 1957.
James, Henry. *Portraits of Places*. London, 1883.
Jones, Ernest. *The Life and Work of Sigmund Freud*. London, 1954.
Jones, Henry Festing. *Diversions in Sicily*. London, 1909.

188

References

Keun, Odette. *I Discover the English*. London, 1934.

Kipling, Rudyard. *Souvenirs of France*. London, 1933.

Kohl, Ida. *Paris und die Franzosen*. Berlin, 1845.

Kohl, Hans. *The Mind of Germany*. New York, 1960.

Kriegel, Annie. *Les Communistes Français*. Paris, 1968.

Laurens, Anne. *Britain is no Island*. London, 1967.

Lawrence, D. H. *England My England*. London, 1924.

Lawrence, D. H. *Sea and Sardinia*. London, 1923.

Lawrence, D. H. *Twilight in Italy*. London, 1916.

Le Blanc, Abbé. *Letters on the English and French Nations*. London, 1747.

Lechat, Paul. *Italie*. Paris, 1954.

Le Play, Pierre. *Voyage en Allemagne et en Belgique*. Paris, 1821.

Letts, Malcolm. *As The Foreigner Saw Us*. London, 1935.

Locke, P. J. (ed.). *European Business Correspondence and Practice*. London, 1967.

Lubbock, Percy. *Roman Pictures*. London, 1923.

McKay, Donald. *The United States and France*. Cambridge, Mass., 1951.

Malaparte, Curzio, *Corriere della Sera*, passim, 1935

Mann, Thomas. *Doktor Faustus*. New York, 1941.

Marandon, Sylvaine. *L'Image de la France dans l'Angleterre Victorienne*. Paris, 1967.

Martin, L. *L'Anglais est-il un Juif?* Paris, 1896.

Maurois, André. *Les Discours du Docteur O'Grady*. Paris, 1922.

Maurois, André. *Les Nouveaux Discours du Docteur O'Grady*. Paris, 1950.

Maurois, André. *Les Silences du Colonel Bramble*. Paris, 1921.

Maurras, Charles. *L'Action Française*, passim, 1909, 1914.

Mawson, Christian (ed.). *Portrait of England*. London, 1942.

Mayer, Tony. *La Vie Anglaise*. Paris, 1959.

Mayne, Richard. "Any More for the Stereotype?", *Encounter*, Vol. XXVII, No. 2, August, 1966.

Mayne, Richard. "Better in France?", *Encounter*, Vol. XXIII, No. 5, November, 1964.

Mayne, Richard. *Cardinal Humbert of Silva Candida*. Unpublished Ph.D. thesis, Cambridge, 1955.

Mayne, Richard. *The Community of Europe*. London, 1962; New York, 1963.

Mayne, Richard. "France 1969", *The Listener*, June 26, 1969.

Mayne, Richard. "Italian Notebook", *Encounter*, Vol. XXIII, No. 4, October 1964.

Mayne, Richard. *The Recovery of Europe*. London/New York, 1970.

Mayne, Richard. "The Year the Fifties Ended", *Sunday Times Magazine*, December 14, 1969.

Meister, J. H. *Souvenirs de mes voyages en Angleterre*. Paris, 1791.

Mélinette, R. *Instantanées d'Allemagne*. Paris, 1896.

Mendelssohn, Felix. *Letters from Italy and Switzerland*. Transl. Mary Wallance, IIIrd ed., London, 1864.

Meredith, George. *One of Our Conquerors*. London, 1891.

Meredith, George. *Up To Midnight*. London, 1873.

Michelet, Jules. *Voyage en Allemagne*. Paris, 1842.

Middleton, Drew. *The British*. London, 1963.

Midgley, John. *Germany*. London, 1968.

Mikes, George. *How to Be an Alien*. London, 1946.

Mikes, George. *How to Be Inimitable*. London, 1960.

Mikes, George. *How to Unite Nations*. London, 1963.

Mikes, George. *Italy for Beginners*. London, 1956.

Mikes, George. *Little Cabbages*. London, 1955.

Mikes, George. *Ueber Alles*. London, 1953.

Montagu, Lady Mary Wortley. *Travel Letters*. London, 1763.

Montaigne, Michel de. *Essais*. Paris, 1580-88.

Morand, Paul. *Hiver Caraïbe*. Paris, 1921.

Morley, Henry (ed.), *The Spectator*. London, 1868.

Murry, John Middleton. *Love, Freedom, and Society*. London, 1957.

Nicolson, Harold. *Diplomacy*. 2nd ed. Oxford, 1950.

Nietzsche, Friedrich. *Götzen-Dämmerung*. Leipzig, 1889.

Nietzsche, Friedrich. *Jenseits von Gut und Böse*. Basel, 1886.

Nourissier, François. *The French*. Transl. Adrienne Foulke, London, 1970.

Orwell, George. *Inside the Whale and Other Essays*. New ed., London, 1962.

Pickles, Dorothy. *France*. London, 1964.

Planchais, Jean (ed.) *Les Provinciaux*. Paris, 1970.

Plumyene, Jean & Lasierra, Raymond (ed.). *Le Sottisier de l'Europe*. Paris, 1970.

References

Political and Economic Planning. *Young Europeans in England.* London, 1962.

Praz, Mario. *The Flaming Heart.* New York, 1958.

Priouret, Roger. *Les Managers Européens.* Paris, 1970.

Pückler-Muskau, Prince. *Letters.* Ed. E. M. Butler, London, 1957.

Reader's Digest European Surveys.

Renan, Ernest. *Voyage en Italie.* Paris, 1849.

Renier, G. J. *The English: Are They Human?* London, 1931.

Revel, J.-F. *En France.* Paris, 1965.

Revel, J.-F. *Pour l'Italie.* Paris, 1958.

Rhodes, Albert. *Monsieur at Home.* London, 1885.

Rogers, Samuel. *Italian Journal.* Ed. J. R. Hale, London, 1956.

Rogers, Samuel. *Italy.* London, 1830.

Rolland, Romain. *Lettre à Clare Collet*, April 1, 1905.

Rudorff, Raymond. *The Myth of France.* London, 1970.

Ruskin, John. *The Stones of Venice.* London, 1851-53.

Sampson, Anthony. *The New Anatomy of Britain.* London, 1971.

Schoenbrun, David. *As France Goes.* London, 1957.

Schopenhauer, Arthur. *Werke.* Leipzig, 1891-2.

Shelley, Mary W. *Frankenstein.* London, 1818.

Shelley, P. B. *Letter to T. L. Peacock*, April 20, 1818.

Shonfield, Andrew. "The Pragmatic Illusion", *Encounter*, Vol. XXVIII, No. 12. June, 1967.

Siegfried, André. *L'Ame des peuples.* Paris, 1950.

Smedts, M. *Engeland.* Amsterdam, 1964.

Smollett, Tobias. *Travels Through France and Italy.* New ed., London, 1919.

Stanley, Arthur (ed.). *Under Italian Skies.* London, 1950.

Stendhal. *Chroniques italiennes.* New ed., Paris, 1964.

Stendhal. *Journal de Londres.* Paris, 1817.

Sterne, Laurence. *A Sentimental Journey.* London, 1768.

Stoker, Bram. *Dracula.* London, 1897.

Symonds, J. A. *New Italian Sketches.* Leipzig, 1884.

Taine, Hippolyte. *Notes sur l'Angleterre.* Paris, 1872.

Taine, Hippolyte. *Voyage en Italie.* Paris, 1866.

Taylor, Bayard. *At Home and Abroad.* New York, 1860.

Thackeray, W. M. *Essays in Punch.* London, 1849.

Thackeray, W. M. *The History of the Next French Revolution.* London, 1844.

Thackeray, W. M. *The Paris Sketch Book.* London, 1840.

Thomson, David. *Democracy in France since 1870.* 5th ed., London, 1969.

Tissot, V. *L'Allemagne amoureuse.* Paris, 1884.

Tracy, G.-M. *Les Anglais parlent des Français.* Paris/Geneva, 1968.

Treves, G. A. *The Golden Ring.* Transl. Sylvia Sprigge, London, 1956.

Trollope, T. A. *What I Remember.* London, 1887.

Vallès, Jules. *La Rue à Londres.* Paris, 1876-7.

Vignola, A. *Toutes les femmes.* Paris, 1874.

Villa, Paul-Michel. *L'Angleterre: un monde à l'envers.* Paris, 1967.

Voltaire, François Marie Arouet de. *Lettres philosophiques.* Paris, 1734.

Walpole, Horace. *The Castle of Otranto.* London, 1764.

Webster, John. *The Duchess of Malfi.* London, 1623.

Webster, John. *The White Devil.* London, 1612.

Weimann, Charles. *Les Deux races.* Paris, 1918.

Wilson, Harold. *The Labour Government 1964-70.* London, 1971.

Wilson, John Dover (ed.). *Life in Shakespeare's England.* Cambridge, 1911.

Wollaston, G. H. (ed.). *The Englishman in Italy.* Oxford, 1909.

Young, Arthur. *Travels in France and Italy.* London, 1792.

6 Cosmopolitans

Browning, Oscar, et al. *Picturesque Europe.* London, n.d.

Coombes, David. *Politics and Bureaucracy in the European Community.* London, 1970.

The Economist.

Einzig, Paul. *The Euro-Dollar System.* London, 1964.

Einzig, Paul. *Foreign Dollar Loans in Europe.* London, 1965.

European Communities. *General Reports.* Brussels/Luxembourg, annual.

L'Expansion.

L'Express.

Grubel, Herbert G. *The International Monetary System.* London, 1969.

Hirsch, Fred. *Money International.* New ed., London, 1969.

Lerner, Daniel & Gorden, Morton. *Euratlantica: Changing Perspectives of European Elites.* Cambridge, Mass., 1969.

Lewis, Norman. *The Honoured Society.* London, 1964.

References

McCreary, Edward A. *The Americanization of Europe*. New York, 1964.

Mayne, Richard. *The Institutions of the European Community*. London, 1968.

Neuvecelle, Jean. *Eglise capitale Vatican*. Paris, 1954.

Pantaleone, Michele. *The Mafia in Politics*. London, 1966.

Perissich, Riccardo. *Gli eurocrati tra realtà e mitologia*. Bologna, 1970.

Randall, Sir Alec. *Vatican Assignment*. London, 1956.

Romano, Salvatore F. *Storia della Mafia*. Milan, 1963.

Sampson, Anthony. *The New Europeans*. London, 1968.

Time.

Vernay, Alain. *Les Paradis fiscaux*. Paris, 1968.

7 A European Identity

Hay, Denys. Europe: *The Emergence of an Idea*. Edinburgh, 1957.

Mayne, Richard. *The Community of Europe*. London, 1962; New York, 1963.

Mayne, Richard. *The Recovery of Europe*. London/New York, 1970.

Mayne, Richard (ed.). *Europe Tomorrow*. London, 1972.

Rougemont, Denis de. *The Idea of Europe*. New York, 1968.

Rougemont, Denis de. *Lettre ouverte aux Européens*. Paris, 1970.

Index

Index

Index

Index

Index

ice ages 16–17, 30, 33–4, 35
Iceland 17, 18, 19, 46, 47, 56
Icelandic language 54
Ido 57
Illyrians 41
Imperial Preference 149
inconstancy 98
India 41, 43
Indians 43
individualism 104, 113–14
"Indo-European" language 53–4
Industrial Revolution 116, 149
Institute for Strategic Studies 164
insularity 121, 146–7
intelligence, cult of 105, 115–16
interbreeding 48
Interglossa 57
Interlaken 124
international business 160–1
International Monetary Fund 7
International Ruhr Authority 169
Interpol 162
inventions 6
Iolanthe 7
Iraq 35, 36
Ireland 14, 15, 36, 47
Irish language 54
iron ore 23
Isar river 52
Isenree, Dr Emil 102–3
Ispra 163
Istanbul 49
Italian language 54, 67, 68–9
Italia nostra 93–4
Italians, The 90
Italici 41, 54
Italy 9, 19, 23, 24, 29, 31, 32, 38, 40, 41, 43, 44, 46, 47, 48, 49, 59, 60, 117, 149, 153, 154, 158, 163, 178; images of 81–93
Ivoclar Vivadent 110

James, Henry 1, 2, 10, 100, 104, 105
Java 28
Jews 43, 119
Joan of Arc 38, 135
John Bull's Neighbour in Her True Light 103

John Halifax, Gentleman 104
Johnson & Johnson 159
Johnson, Dr Samuel 51, 97
John XXIII, Pope 91
Jordan 35
Journal of a Tour to the Hebrides, The 51
Juan, Don 63–4
Jugoslavia 43, 47, 59, 154, 163
Jutes 42

Kant, Immanuel 78, 127
Karlsruhe 163
Keun, Odette 125, 140
Keyserling Count Hermann Alexander 62, 107, 120
Khrushchev, Nikita 44
kinship 48
Knossos 31
Kohl, Ida 97
Kohn, Hans 75
Adenauer, Konrad 79
Krakatoa 12
Kraus, Karl 61

Labrador Current 17
La Chapelle-aux-Saints 31
La Ferrassie 31   *La Stampa* 91
laisser-faire 4
Lake Distict 14
Lang, Fritz 69
languages 1, 51, 173–4; origin 52
Lapland 47
Lappish language 54
Lapps 42
Lascaux 33
Latin America 3
Latin language 54, 174
Latvia 47, 59
Latvian language 54
lava 12, 22
Lawrence, D. H. 22, 85, 87–9, 91, 92
League of Nations 63
Le Blanc, Abbé 126
Leibniz, Gottfried Wilhelm von 64, 175
Leo XIII, Pope 158
Leopardi, Giacomo 91

200

Index

Les Baux 38
Les Eyzies 32, 33, 37
less developed countries 180, 181
Letzeburgesch language 54, 68, 164
Levalloisians 33
Levant, The 56
Liechtenstein 157, 159–60
Linate airport 81
Lindisfarne gospels 136
linguistic minorities 59–61, 156
Lithuania 56, 58, 59
Lithuanian language 54
Loire river 24
Lombardy 147
London 81, 138, 139
loquacity 97–8, 108
Loren, Sophia 46
Lorraine 23, 71, 155
Los Millares 36, 38
Louis XIV 149
Low Countries 15, 39, 58
Lubitsch, Ernst 138
Lucania 93
Lucerne 124
Luther, Martin 76
Luxembourg 23, 112, 155, 160–1, 163, 164–5; image of 151, 144
Lyon, Margot 163

McCarthy, Mary 110
Macedonian language 54
Machiavelli, Niccolò 82
McKay, Donald 107
Macmillan, Harold 142
Mâcon 34
Madame Bovary 100
Madariaga, Don Salvador de 63–6, 68, 69, 133
Maes Howe 38
Magdalenians 33
Maggiore, Lake 81
Magyar language 54
Magyars 42
Mainz 4
Malaparte, Curzio 123
Mallet-Joris, Françoise 156
Mallia 36
Malta 22, 36, 44; cabbages in 23
Mann, Thomas 74

Marceau, Félicien 156
Marconi, Guglielmo 6, 91
Marianne 98
Marigny, Antoine 175
Marks and Spencer 23
marriages, dynastic 58
Mars 1
Marseille 162
Massif Central 15, 47
"Mauer mandible" 29
Maurras, Charles 72, 110, 119
May 1968 *événements* 117
Mayo 14
Mazzini, Guiseppe 2, 9
Medici family 90, 91
Mediterranean sea 15, 17, 18, 20, 21, 23, 25, 29, 35, 36, 38, 40, 41, 44; supposed land bridges 29
"Mediterranean" people 45–6, 49
megaliths 38–9
Mendelssohn, Felix 84
Meredith, George 96, 97
Mers-el-Kebir 136
Meseta 16
Messina 12
metalinguistics 61
metallurgy 35–6, 39
Mexico 17, 36, 162
Michelangelo Buonarotti 63
Michelet, Jules 73
Middle East 3, 35–6
Middle West 17
Midlands 23
migrant workers 156–7
Mikes, George 74
Milan 92–3
minerals 23
Mitteleuropa 172
Modification, La 125
Monaco 32, 155, 157–9
Monde, Le 119
Mongols 42, 43
monkeys 28
Monnet, Jean 164, 166
Montagu, Lady Mary Wortley 102, 146–7
Montaigne, Michel Eyquem de 83
Mont Blanc 12
Monte Carlo 157–9

Index

Index

soil 20–2
Solutré 34
South Tyrol 59, 60, 155
sovereignty, delegation of 7–8
Spaak, Charles 156
Spaak, Paul-Henri 156
Spain 1, 16, 19, 23, 29, 36, 38, 40, 42, 43, 46, 47, 58, 59, 63, 112, 137, 154; image of 151
Spanish language 54, 63, 64, 69
Spectator, The 84
speech-tunes 49, 54
Speed, John 98
Spektrum Europas, Das 62
Spinelli, Altiero 169
Spock, Dr Benjamin 92
spring wheat 23
Stalin, Svetlana 160
Stampa, La 91
Star Carr 35
statues 5
Steinheim 30
Stendhal (Henri Beyle) 130, 132
Sterne, Laurence 101
Stoker, Bram 83
Stonehenge 36, 39
Strabo 24
Strasbourg 155, 163
street names 6
Sturzo, Don Luigi 91
Sully, Duc de 126, 175
supranationalism 169
Sutton Hoo burial 136
Swanscombe 30
Sweden 13, 22, 23, 38, 41, 43, 47, 58, 59, 69, 112, 160; image of 151
Swedenborg, Emanuel 121
Swedish language 54, 69
Swift, Jonathan 70
Swiss 76
Switzerland 1, 16, 47, 59, 112, 124, 160, 162; image of 151
Syria 35, 36, 40, 136

taciturnity 127–8, 139
Tacitus 78
Taine, Hippolyte 83, 89, 128, 129, 130

Tardenoisians 33
taste, aesthetic 86
Tati Jacques 168
Tatra mountains 15
Tawney, R. H. 172
Taylor, Bayard 74, 75, 89, 124
technology and frontiers 7
teeth 44, 49
Tell Murebat 36
temperature of the earth 11–12
temperatures in Europe 17
Tenda hunting grounds 59
"Teutonic" people 45–6, 49
Thackeray, William Makepeace 100, 101 , 103 , 113
Thames river 30
Thirty Years' War 78
This Way Please 123–4
Thomson, James 18
Times, The 137
tools 26, 27
Torralba 29
Totò 92
tourists 154–5
trade-routes 41
translator's slang 6
Transylvania 83
travel 5, 25, 70
Treatise on the Origin of Language 62
Trollope, Thomas Adolphus 87
Tula coalfield 23
Tunisia 29
Turin 93
Turkey 35, 36
Turkish Straits 29, 38
Turks 42, 43
Tuscany 40

ugliness 102, 130
Ukraine 39
Ukrainian language 54
Ulster 1, 14
Union of Soviet Socialist Republics (USSR) 14, 23, 59, 178–9
United Nations 149
United States of America (USA) 1, 5, 9, 17, 23, 45, 56, 61, 63, 80,

Index